Lục Xì

Southeast Asia

POLITICS, MEANING, AND MEMORY

David Chandler and Rita Smith Kipp

SERIES EDITORS

Lục Xì

Prostitution and Venereal

Disease in Colonial Hanoi

VŨ TRỌNG PHỤNG

Translated, with an introduction, by
SHAUN KINGSLEY MALARNEY

UNIVERSITY OF HAWAI'I PRESS   *Honolulu*

© 2011 University of Hawai'i Press

All rights reserved

Printed in the United States of America

16 15 14 13 12 11   6 5 4 3 2 1

Library of Congress Cataloging-in-Publication Data

Vu, Trong Phung, 1912–1939.

Luc xì : prostitution and venereal disease in colonial Hanoi / by Vu Trong Phung ; translated, with an introduction, by Shaun Kingsley Malarney.

p. cm. — (Southeast Asia: politics, meaning, and memory)

Includes bibliographical references and index.

ISBN 978-0-8248-3467-8 (hardcover : alk. paper)

1. Prostitution—Vietnam—Hanoi—History.   2. Prostitutes—Vietnam—Hanoi—Social conditions.   I. Malarney, Shaun Kingsley.   II. Title.   III. Series: Southeast Asia—politics, meaning, memory.

HQ242.5.H36V8 2011

363.4′405973—dc22

2010034644

University of Hawai'i Press books are printed on acid-free paper and meet the guidelines for permanence and durability of the Council on Library Resources.

Series designed by Richard Hendel

Printed by Edwards Brothers, Inc.

CONTENTS

ACKNOWLEDGMENTS

I have been fortunate in the course of completing this translation to have been the beneficiary of a great deal of support and assistance. My university, International Christian University, granted me sabbatical leaves in 2001–2002 and 2009–2010 that allowed me to conduct the primary research in Hanoi and complete the final manuscript. The Centre for Vietnamese Studies in Hanoi provided logistical support in arranging visas and access to research facilities. The staff of the Vietnamese National Archives I in Hanoi was also gracious in providing me access to the colonial-era files I needed. I am not by training a professional translator, but Stephen Snyder and John Nathan, both of whom have extensive experience translating Japanese literature, were generous in sharing their thoughts and ideas about translation. Nguyễn Tấn Lan Thy worked through the complete text with me and helped with difficult translations. Olga Dror, Lisa Drummond, Tine Gammeltoft, Greg Shaya, and especially Laurence Monnais provided helpful suggestions, ideas, and clarifications. Pamela Kelley, David Chandler, Rita Kipp, Ann Ludeman, Bojana Ristich, and the staff of the University of Hawai'i Press were very helpful moving the project forward. My late wife Christy was an early encourager of the project, and my son Liêm helped prepare the photographs. Finally, Peter Zinoman and Nguyễn Nguyệt Cầm, the translators of Phụng's novel *Dumb Luck,* introduced me to the text and provided innumerable constructive ideas and suggestions. My deepest thanks to all.

TRANSLATOR'S NOTE

Lục Xì was originally published in eleven installments in the Hanoi newspaper *Tương Lai* (Future) from January to April 1937. Soon after publication, Vũ Trọng Phụng prepared the text for publication as a book but only after significant revisions that involved the addition, deletion, and rearrangement of a number of passages. Since its first publication in book form by the Minh Phương publishing house in late 1937, the text has been reedited and republished on several occasions by other publishers, some of whom relied upon manuscripts that were missing pages. This multiplicity of texts, as well as the absence of an original unedited manuscript or statement from Phụng that clearly identifies one particular text as the definitive version, requires the translator to make a judgment regarding which texts and passages to include in a translation. In an effort to remain as faithful as possible to what I would regard as Phụng's conception of the definitive version, I have based this translation upon the version published in book form. However, I have relied upon two published versions of the text, one published in 1999 in *Vũ Trọng Phụng: Toàn Tập, Tập I: Phóng Sự* (Vũ Trọng Phụng: The Complete Works, Volume 4: *Reportages*) (see Vũ Trọng Phụng 1999) and another published in 2000 in *Phóng Sự Việt Nam, 1932–1945* (Vietnamese *Reportage*, 1932–1945) (see Phan Trọng Thưởng, Nguyễn Cừ, and Nguyễn Hữu Sơn 2000). Both of these versions were assembled by Vietnamese experts on Phụng and *reportage*. They are almost completely identical to each other, as well as to earlier published versions, but each has its interesting additions and deletions. In the interest of completeness, I have presented all of the passages that appear in both of the published versions, as I think that will bring the reader closest to Phụng's original intentions. The passages that appear in only one version are footnoted in the text. Despite these efforts at completeness, there are still several sentences that remain vague or unclear, such as Phụng's insertion of a quotation in chapter 10 from Dr. H. Coppin in which Coppin states that he will explain something later but no explanation follows. These sentences unfortunately cannot be clarified, and they have been translated as they are found in the original text.

A second challenge is the issue of Phụng's translations of French texts and terms into Vietnamese. Throughout the text, though particularly in chapter 10, "The Authorities' Perspective," Phụng draws extensively on the publications of a number of French doctors and officials who professionally dealt with the prostitution and venereal disease problems in colonial Hanoi. Almost all of these authors had served as directors of Hanoi's Municipal Dispensary, and most of their writings were published in the *Bulletin de la Société Médico-Chirurgicale de l'Indochine*. Phụng included many translations from their work, some of which are several pages long. Phụng had a great deal of experience as a translator, but a close reading of his translations and the French originals reveals that he took some minor liberties, most likely due to haste. I have not tried to correct these liberties but have translated his translations as he wrote them. In most cases, however, I was able to locate the original text and have provided footnotes for interested readers. Another translation issue relates to Phụng's rendering of the "Service des Moeurs." In the text, Phụng glosses this with the vernacular Vietnamese expression Cảnh Sát Xướng Kỹ, which can literally be rendered as the "Singing Girls' Police." Phụng employed "police" instead of "service"; therefore in the text I have translated the term with the commonly used French expression "Police des Moeurs." It should be noted that French writers, be they doctors or officials, tended to use these two terms interchangeably, even though "Service des Moeurs" is the more accurate term.

A final complexity relates to translating the critical term "prostitute." One interesting theme that runs throughout *Lục Xì* is the question of which term is the most appropriate. In the text, Phụng uses three different terms, each with its own unique semantics. The coarsest, which Phụng uses the most frequently, is *đĩ*, which I have translated as "prostitute." A second, more polite term is *kỹ nữ*, most commonly translated as "courtesan." The final term is *gái giang hồ*, the most euphemistic of the three. *Giang hồ* is a poetic term for a city's pleasure quarters, normally rendered in French as the *demi-monde*. Given that *gái* is the term for female, *gái giang hồ* could be glossed as "women of the *demi-monde*," but in the interest of parsimony, I use the French translation of the expression, *demi-mondaine*. These different usages are essential to understanding Phụng's discussion of prostitutes and prostitution, as well as the women's own feelings about the different terms; thus throughout the text these terms are translated in exact accordance with Phụng's own usages.

INTRODUCTION

Vũ Trọng Phụng and the Anxieties of "Progress"

Shaun Kingsley Malarney

"If we are genuinely concerned about our society and our race, then we must honestly understand the causes of our fears and anxieties." It was with these words that Vũ Trọng Phụng challenged his more timid readers at the end of the introductory chapter to his classic 1937 *reportage* on prostitution and venereal disease in colonial Hanoi, *Lục Xì*. Phụng did indeed have many worries and fears. By the late 1930s the city of Hanoi, which had by that point been under French colonial control for over fifty years, had a vast commercial sex industry. According to contemporary estimates, the city of some 180,000 people had 5,000 women working as prostitutes; to Phụng such a figure meant that one of every thirty-five residents was apparently ready and willing to spread venereal disease among the population. In the city center Hanoi had a secretive medical facility, known in French as the Dispensaire Municipal (Municipal Dispensary) and in Vietnamese as the Nhà Lục Xì (discussed below), where prostitutes were examined for venereal disease and, if infected, held until they were cured. Hanoi also had high rates of infection for venereal disease, which exacted a painful and sometimes deadly toll on men and women, young and old, European and Vietnamese. Ultimately, however, these realities led to a troubling question that animated Phụng's thinking throughout *Lục Xì:* what did the existence of this enormous industry and its tragic consequences say about the state of Vietnamese society and culture in the late 1930s?

Prostitution, and the masses of women infected with sexually transmitted diseases that often accompany it, have in different societies and different historical moments become the foci for the articulation of broader social concerns, especially concerns about sociocultural breakdown or decay. As the French historian Alain Corbin wrote of nineteenth-century French prostitution, "What was written and said about prostitution was then a focus for collective delusions and a meeting point for all manner of anxieties" (quoted in Hershatter 1999, 5). In the French case those concerns were linked to such issues as "immorality," social revolution, and male mastery, yet in the case of Shanghai in the late nineteenth- and twentieth-century cases analyzed by Gail Hershatter (1999, 4–7), the discourse surrounding prostitution at certain times elaborated on such concerns as moral danger, national decay, and gender relationships. Regarding venereal disease, Megan Vaughan (1991, 129–154) has compellingly described how in colonial Buganda a syphilis epidemic became a powerful metaphor for concerns about the loss of control over female sexuality, while Nguyễn-võ Thu-hương (2008) has demonstrated the ways in which discussions about HIV-AIDS in contemporary Vietnam articulate concerns about national decay and the consequences of economic liberalization.[1]

For Vũ Trọng Phụng, the complex reality of prostitution and venereal disease was the source and focus of a number of profound anxieties about the sociocultural status quo in colonial Hanoi. As he clearly recognized, Vietnam's colonial encounter with French culture and civilization was couched in the rhetoric of "progress": through their encounter with the allegedly superior French civilization, the ostensibly backward and inferior society and culture of the Vietnamese were to improve and progress. However, while five decades of colonial contact had certainly produced changes in Vietnamese society and culture, Phụng openly questioned the idea that they had been changes for the better or that they had come without a cost. As I shall argue in this introduction, in *Lục Xì* Phụng conducts a remarkable analysis of prostitution and venereal disease, but in doing so, he also compellingly makes the case that the social problems that they both represented and generated were themselves symptoms of much deeper problems that had been developing in colonial Vietnamese society and that challenged the notion that Vietnam was progressing under colonial rule.

VŨ TRỌNG PHỤNG AND THE BACKGROUND TO *LỤC XÌ*

Many Vietnamese regard Vũ Trọng Phụng as one of the most gifted writers of the twentieth century. Born in Hanoi in 1912, Phụng was an only child raised by his mother after his father died from tuberculosis seven months after his birth. Growing up in poverty, he completed primary school but was unable to continue formal schooling past the age of fourteen. In his late teens, he began publishing short fiction and soon after embarked upon a career as a journalist as well. By the time of his death from tuberculosis and opium addiction in 1939, just one week before his twenty-seventh birthday, Phụng had compiled an impressive literary output that included "at least eight novels, seven plays, five book-length works of nonfiction reportage, several dozen short stories, a handful of lengthy literary translations, and hundreds of reviews, essays, articles, and editorials" (Zinoman 2002, 1).[2]

Phụng's fiction writings earned him tremendous acclaim, but he was equally renowned for his investigative journalism and would later be known as the "Northern King of *Reportage*" (Ông Vua Phóng Sự Đất Bắc). *Reportage*, which can be described as a form of social-realist investigative journalism, had become a popular form of journalistic writing in Vietnam in the 1930s. Inspired by writers in France and other nations, Vietnamese journalists began publishing *reportages* in the early 1930s. Over the following decade and a half *reportage* took a number of different forms, such as travelogues from locales across Vietnam, reflective pieces on social and cultural life, or descriptions of contemporary events such as village life or festivals, but it acquired its quintessential form and achieved tremendous popularity after the 1932 publication of Tam Lang's remarkable work, *Tôi Kéo Xe* (I Pulled a Rickshaw).[3] *Tôi Kéo Xe* possessed many of the characteristics that came to define Vietnamese-language *reportage* in the 1930s. The story involved the author, a journalist for the Hanoi newspaper *Hà Thành Ngọ Báo* (Hanoi Midday News), working as a rickshaw puller in order to learn about and then describe to his readers the lives and experiences of the people in this occupation. Written in the first person, with direct quotations and rich descriptions of the difficult and sometimes brutal experiences that rickshaw pullers endured, the story caused an immediate sensation after its publication. Peter Zinoman (2002, 17) notes that it had a strong impact on Phụng's later devotion to *reportage*.

Tôi Kéo Xe had several other characteristics that would come to characterize *reportage* and Phụng's work. In terms of its subjects, *reportage* often focused on the marginal, disenfranchised, dispossessed, unseen, or even exploited members of Vietnamese society. A survey of the contents of the three-volume set *Phóng Sự Việt Nam, 1931–1945* (Vietnamese *Reportage, 1931–1945*; see Phan Trọng Thưởng, Nguyễn Cừ, and Nguyễn Hữu Sơn 2000) reveals pieces on such diverse individuals as herbal medicine doctors, farmers, prostitutes, taxi-girls, laborers, and criminals. In writing *reportage*, journalists often deliberately sought out groups or individuals that were outside society's mainstream and were looked down upon by the elite. The latter point is significant because *reportage* writing tended to be sympathetic toward its subjects. *Reportage* writers were supposed to provide an accurate factual accounting of the groups or issues they investigated, but the tone was to be measured and not of a salacious or tabloid-type nature. Of course, this was the ideal, and some writers, including Phụng himself and the author Việt Sinh (whom he mentions in the text), were accused of failing to live up to this ethic. Finally, *reportages* were also often linked to broader reform agendas. Many *reportages* attempted to objectively describe the problems colonial Vietnamese society faced and then accompanied these descriptions with suggestions about possible solutions. The emergence of this type of critical and advocacy-oriented journalism in the 1930s was truly innovative, but as Greg Lockhart (1996, 1) has noted, it fell out of favor with the authorities after the revolution in 1945.

Phụng published his first *reportage* in 1933. Entitled *Cạm Bẫy Người* (The Man Trap), it examined the infrastructure of and problems caused by gambling. In the following years he wrote several more, the most noteworthy being the 1934 *Kỹ Nghệ Lấy Tây* (The Industry of Marrying Europeans), which examined the complex relations between Vietnamese women and French men, particularly soldiers; *Cơm Thầy Cơm Cô* (Household Servants), a 1936 publication that discussed the lives of household servants in Hanoi; and *Lục Xì* in 1937.[4] Stylistically, all of his works explore social problems or concerns, focus on the lives of the dispossessed or marginalized, collect material through firsthand reporting, and employ first-person commentary or quotations from interviewees to give a lived immediacy to the text. Phụng himself looms large in all his texts, yet his dry wit, keen sense of irony, and willingness to place himself in extraordinary circumstances—such as hiring himself out as a domestic worker in *Cơm Thầy Cơm Cô* or the remarkable evening he spent in a hotel room interviewing two prostitutes in *Lục Xì*—gave his *reportage* a unique flair.

Phụng published *Lục Xì* in eleven installments in the Hanoi newspaper *Tương Lai* (Future) from January through April 1937.[5] His ability to gain entry into the Municipal Dispensary during early February of that year was due to the willingness of the Hanoi municipal government to grant journalists entry for the first time, but his interests in the Dispensary, prostitution, and the social problems they involved can be traced back further. To understand Phụng's position, it is important to note that neither prostitution nor venereal disease were concealed topics in Hanoi in the late 1930s. As will be detailed below, there was a burgeoning commercial sex industry in the city at the time, the colonial and municipal governments had long focused on both subjects as areas of concern and policy reform, the popular press often featured discussions of them, and the city's newspapers and public spaces had significant numbers of advertisements directing consumers to various establishments for venereal disease treatment. Phụng parodied the latter in his renowned 1936 novel *Số Đỏ* (Dumb Luck), in which the protagonist, Red Haired Xuân, is temporarily employed to publicly advertise the medicaments of the "King of Cochinchinese Venereal Disease Treatment" through a loudspeaker (see Vũ Trọng Phụng 2002). Stated simply, prostitution and venereal disease were openly visible and engaged in the public sphere.

If one were to believe some of Phụng's contemporary and later critics, his interest in these topics derived from a deeper interest in the lewd and pornographic, a trait they claimed was visible in his work (see Vũ Trọng Phụng 2000a, 275–298). This characterization, however, was a serious misrepresentation of his goals in publicly addressing these problems, a point most evident in the text that can be regarded as the fictional prelude to *Lục Xì,* the October 1936 novel *Làm Đĩ* (Prostitute). Similar to others of his novels, *Làm Đĩ* is a work of social-realist fiction set in Hanoi in the late 1930s. The novel's protagonist is a woman named Huyền, and the novel addresses a question that Phụng explores in *Lục Xì:* how women became prostitutes. Huyền is the daughter of an elite family; despite all of the advantages of her birth, she experiences a series of events that lead her into prostitution. The text is centered around an encounter in an upscale brothel involving Huyền, the narrator, and his good friend Qúy, all of whom have known each other since they were young students. After meeting her again as a prostitute in the beginning of the book, the narrator asks the following:

"But why was she corrupted?

"Why has the child of an upstanding family, who did not lack for education, come to be a prostitute?" (Vũ Trọng Phụng 2000a, 72)

The narrator presses Huyền on this question, and in the remainder of the narrative she answers it through a detailed recounting of her life that she has inscribed in a diary. As the story proceeds, it is clear that Phụng eschews a simplistic monocausal explanation and instead emphasizes a number of factors in her recruitment to prostitution, such as "romanticism," materialism, the relaxation of rules regarding male-female interaction, the absence of sexual education, the prohibition of marriage among lineage mates, arranged marriage, and the inequalities and denial of human feeling the latter two practices could involve. The inclusion of these factors brings out a tension in Phụng's approach to the issue in that it is simultaneously critical of preexisting practices (such as the last four factors noted) and recent social changes (such as the initial three factors). It also demonstrates that for Phụng, the path to prostitution involves multiple factors; perhaps more important in Huyền's case, it was a decision due to desperation and a lack of other feasible options. One can fairly argue that Huyền makes the choice to become a prostitute, and indeed she accepts prostitution as the only solution to the problem she faces near the narrative's end, but Phụng's construction of her biography in the novel quietly asserts that it was the broader array of sociological factors that placed her in the position in which prostitution was the only feasible option left to her. Society, at a significant level, shared some responsibility for her becoming a prostitute. Phụng's tone in *Làm Đĩ* evinces a profound sympathy for Huyền. Indeed, there is a measure of similarity between her and Thúy Kiều, the heroine of Nguyễn Du's classic nineteenth-century epic poem *The Tale of Kiều*, to which Phụng repeatedly refers in *Lục Xì* (see Nguyễn Du 1983). In both cases a beautiful, talented woman from an upstanding family endures a life of indignities and suffering, notably in the form of prostitution, due to forces beyond her control, and it is each woman's status as a victim of outside forces that allows the reader to remain sympathetic to her because she is fundamentally blameless.

According to an account that Phụng published in May 1938, a combination of pressures at his newspaper to write a new *reportage*, his own desires to write a *reportage* that would have unassailable truths, and his editor's recognition that a *reportage* with "that horrible name" *Lục Xì* would sell papers all provided a stimulus for embarking upon the writing of *Lục Xì* in the months after *Làm Đĩ* was published (Vũ Trọng Phụng 1938, 3). Nevertheless, it is clear that many of the thoughts he engaged in the earlier volume remained fresh in his mind. In turning to *Lục Xì*, however, Phụng moves out of the realm of fictional speculation and into the lives of real prostitutes. He also broadens his focus to include the human costs of prostitution, particularly the consequences of venereal disease in contemporary social life and the experiences of women in the Dispensary. In all of this, Phụng reveals deeper anxieties about the state of Vietnamese society. In order to fully explain those anxieties, more background to the Dispensary and the venereal disease problem is necessary.

THE DISPENSARY AND ITS ROLE IN COLONIAL HANOI

At the time of *Lục Xì*'s writing, the Municipal Dispensary sat at the corner of rue Rodier and boulevard Rollandes (today's Yết Thị and Hai Bà Trưng) in central Hanoi. The building had opened in 1926, following a controversy that Phụng describes, and was near the city's courthouse, the Maison Centrale or Hỏa Lò Prison, and the Hospital for the Indigenous Residents of the Protectorate (l'Hôpital Indigène du Protectorat; hereafter Hôpital Indigène). The existence of a Dispensary in Hanoi dates back to the earliest days of the French presence. The city of Hanoi was officially established as a municipality on July 19, 1888, and on December 21,1888, the Hanoi Municipal Council passed legislation to regulate prostitution; it included a Dispensary as an integral part of the system (the coastal city of Haiphong had passed similar legislation in April 1886) (RST 73684). Hanoi's first dispensary was constructed in early 1889 on the route de la Pagode du Grand Buddha (present-day Quan Thánh). This makeshift structure, made of thatch and bamboo, was destroyed in a typhoon in mid-July of that year. At this point, however, an unsettling association had already begun to develop between the Dispensary and holding facilities for female prisoners as the route de la Pagode du Grand Buddha site had housed both the Dispensary and the women's prison.

At the time of the first dispensary's destruction, city officials were considering a site on the rue des Balances for a more permanent structure (RST 73684), and at some point thereafter a new dispensary was constructed there. This facility was used until 1902, when another new structure was constructed on the route de Hué. This "decent and discreet" facility (Coppin 1930, 571) was closed in December 1915; apparently it was turned into a school, and for the next two years the Dispensary's services were conducted at the Hôpital Indigène (MH 2585 and 2587). In 1918 the city relocated the Dispensary to a former shrine near the mayor's office in the city's center. This "old and insalubrious" facility (Ligue Prophylactique de la Ville de Hanoi 1937, 1) was then replaced with the dispensary constructed in 1926. Regardless of where the dispensaries were located, public health officials were never fully satisfied with them, and they faced a common set of problems. The facilities, for example, rarely had enough beds to accommodate the patients. Dr. H. Coppin (1930, 572) commented that the dispensary near the mayor's office had space for fifty to sixty women but regularly held over one hundred.[6] The 1926 dispensary would face the same problem. Internal amenities were also often lacking. When contemplating the construction of the 1926 facility, the Hanoi administration, then led by Mayor Louis Eckert, had concluded that the existing dispensary "was far from meeting the minimum conditions regarding hygiene and security" (RST 79235), a complaint that had been voiced regarding earlier facilities. Perhaps most troubling was the dispensaries' perceived carceral nature. Officials were very concerned about the seemingly widespread idea that the Dispensary was little more than a prison, and some officials openly articulated that notion. Maurice Cognacq, a doctor who oversaw the Dispensary during his work as a doctor for the city from 1911 through 1916 (he later became lieutenant-governor of Cochinchina), held that for this and other reasons the Dispensary was a site that Vietnamese sought to avoid. He commented in March 1915, "Money is not the only reason that keeps sick women away from the Dispensary. This sanitary establishment is more like a prison; the unfortunates are interned behind solid iron grates as if they were wild animals. The duration of their detention is not compensated for by the treatment they receive, as the treatment of the sick, due to a lack of materials and personnel, is notoriously insufficient" (MH 2585).

Despite these deficiencies, the Dispensary remained a central component in the city's effort to regulate prostitution. In order to understand its role, it is useful to describe the broader legal and administrative context of which it was part. When the Hanoi Municipal Council met on December 5 and 17, 1888, to develop the regulations for prostitution in the city, its deliberations, as would remain the case throughout the colonial period, were profoundly influenced by existing administrative practices in France and its territories. In the early 1800s, the French government had enacted a series of laws designed to create a legal space for the practice of certain types of prostitution. As the historian Jill Harsin has noted (1985, xvi), this legal framework basically accepted that prostitution was going to exist, while it attempted to channel it into particular directions so that its deleterious effects—notably the transmission of venereal diseases—could be reduced if not eliminated. A central component in this system was the officially licensed brothel, or what I will more simply refer to as the licensed brothel, which was known in official parlance as the *maison de tolérance*. (The name itself was revealing, as it indicated that in these houses prostitution was to be tolerated.) When the Hanoi Municipal Council promulgated its 1888 decree, prostitution was allowed to exist, but it could legally be practiced only in licensed brothels. (This law would change in 1891, when independent prostitutes [*femmes isolées*] received official permission to work alone at a locale of their choosing.)[7]

Hanoi's licensed brothels had a number of important features. Their establishment required permission from Hanoi's mayor and the payment of an annual licensing fee *(patente)*, decided upon by the city administration. The proprietors of licensed brothels were required to be female, a regulation that was implemented in order to prevent possible abuses of female prostitutes by male owners (The regulations indeed indicate that those working as prostitutes were expected to be female, but male prostitution did exist into the 1920s and 1930s; see Coppin 1930, 583, and MH 2593). Following regulations issued in 1907, licensed brothels were forbidden to provide alcohol or opium to staff or patrons and could not allow entrance or employment to anyone under the age of eighteen. Of critical importance, women working in licensed brothels were required to register as prostitutes and pay an associated fee at the Hanoi police station, where their names, ages, places of origin, and places of work were recorded in a special register. This requirement was significant because through it the women became classified in French discourse in three ways: *inscrites,* meaning that their names were inscribed in the official register; *filles publiques,* meaning officially recognized prostitutes; or the more commonly used *filles soumises,* which meant that they had submitted to the regulatory regime. As Phụng describes in the text, Vietnamese discourse characterized these women as those who "had papers" *(có giấy).* Once a woman registered, she received a "card" *(carte)* or the "papers" *(giấy)* that allowed her to legally practice her trade.

The Dispensary's primary roles in this system were to monitor the prostitute population for the presence of venereal diseases and then treat those diagnosed with them. After receiving a card to legally practice prostitution, each woman was required to visit the Dispensary once a week for what was described as a "sanitary visit" *(visite sanitaire).* In the late 1930s, Tuesday and Friday mornings were designated for sanitary visits (Charbonnier 1936, 41), although Phụng claims Wednesdays and Fridays were the examination dates. The examination session began around 8 a.m. and lasted for about three hours. During these visits, which Phụng compellingly describes in the text, women had to submit to a gynecological examination to check for visible signs of infection. According to Roger Charbonnier (1936, 42), a French doctor who conducted research on prostitution in Hanoi in the mid-1930s, each examination lasted only a minute or so. If in the course of the exam a woman was suspected of having syphilis, a bacteriological examination was also conducted, though the results were not immediately available. If a woman's examination results were negative, the Dispensary staff wrote "healthy" *(saine)* on her card, and she was free to leave and continue working as a prostitute until her next visit. The coercive nature of the Dispensary came into play if a woman was suspected of having or was diagnosed with a venereal disease. In the former case, the woman was obliged to remain in the Dispensary until the results of her laboratory examinations were returned. If they were negative, she was free to leave, but if a woman was diagnosed with a venereal disease through either clinical observation or a positive bacteriological examination, "unhealthy" *(malsaine)* was written on her card, and she was required to remain in the Dispensary for treatment. This stipulation was first established in Hanoi's 1888 regulations, which required women who were "unhealthy" to remain in the Dispensary until they had "a complete recovery" (Joyeux 1930, 616). A September 1933 report by Dr. Jules Theron, director of the Municipal Hygiene Service and the Dispensary, indicated that for each examination session only 3–5% of the women were required to remain for treatment (MH 2592), a figure that Dr. Bernard Joyeux, who served as Dispensary director for most of the 1930s, placed at approximately 5% the following year (Joyeux 1934b, 903), yet this small percentage had a larger cumulative effect. La Ligue Prophylactique de la Ville de Hanoi (the Prophylactic League of the City of Hanoi; hereafter Prophylactic League) commented in 1937 that the Dispensary often reached its maximum of some 150 patients (1937, 7). It is important to note, however, that the Dispensary's maximum capacity was not reached exclusively with licensed prostitutes. As will be discussed below, Hanoi had a large population of women working as prostitutes illegally. Any woman arrested for illegally practicing prostitution was taken to the Dispensary for a medical examination and required to remain if she received a positive diagnosis for a venereal disease.

The execution of the Dispensary's duties was handled by a staff of nine. The director was always a male European doctor who occupied the position by virtue of being the director of the Municipal Hygiene Service.[8] He was assisted by two "Indochinese doctors" *(médicins indochinois)*, both of whom were male and, as far as the evidence indicates, always Vietnamese.[9] The senior of these two doctors was the director's deputy, who conducted the gynecological examinations in the director's absence. The junior doctor focused on managing the nursing staff, which was composed of two "indigenous nurses" *(infirmières indigènes)*. Over the course of the Dispensary's history all nurses appear to have been both female and Vietnamese. The Dispensary also had a full-time doorman, as well as a pool of guards. Perhaps the most important position for the everyday running of the Dispensary was the "chief supervisor" *(surveillante en chef)*. French colonial medical facilities that had a carceral component, such as the dispensaries and leprosariums, usually appointed full-time European supervisors who lived at the facilities in order to manage them and monitor the patient population. The Dispensary's chief supervisor had always been a European woman, though she was assisted by two female "indigenous supervisors" *(surveillantes indigènes)*, who again appear to have always been Vietnamese. Prior to 1932, the supervisor had for several years been a nun who was a member of the Sisters of Saint Paul of Chartres (RST 78701). The Vietnamese supervisors were also nuns from this order. After 1932, the city administration hired European civilians to serve as chief supervisors, though, as will be discussed below, their professional conduct was at times harmful to the city's goals in operating the facility.

By late 1936 the city administration, working in consultation with such organizations as the Prophylactic League, had completed an ambitious set of reforms in order to improve the Dispensary's physical structure as well as its reputation throughout the city.[10] The admittance of Phụng and other journalists into the Dispensary was part of this agenda. City officials sought to create a new understanding about the Dispensary among city residents, particularly its prostitutes. From the officials' perspective, the term used by Vietnamese to refer to the Dispensary, Lục Xì (or Nhà Lục Xì), had taken on an exclusively negative cast associated with fear, avoidance, and incarceration. Etymologically, the term itself is quite interesting given its obscure and recent origins in the Vietnamese language. The earliest reference to the term that I have located was in an anonymous letter to the Hanoi police written in Vietnamese and dated April 30, 1896; it contains a denunciation of two Vietnamese women who were allegedly working illegally as prostitutes. After denouncing the women, the writer demanded that they be taken to the *lục sì* [sic] for an examination (MH 2579). Given that the first dispensary was set up in 1889, the word was obviously introduced early on. The writings of French doctors in the *Bulletin de la Société Médico-Chirurgicale de l'Indochine* (the journal of a Hanoi-based medical society that had been established in 1907), notably Coppin's 1925 article on prostitution in Hanoi, point to its continued usage, and in the text, Phụng declares to Dr. Joyeux that neither he nor other journalists have any idea about the term's origin. Joyeux comments that it originated from the habit of a jovial French doctor who many years before had performed the medical examinations on Hanoi prostitutes and who at times liked to use English words. According to this explanation, *lục xì* came into use from the doctor asking the women to have a "look-see." Though perhaps fanciful, this remains the most convincing explanation.

The term's obscure etymology aside, by the time of Phụng's writing, *lục xì* was part of the city's everyday vernacular, although elderly Hanoi residents note that it was a coarse word with negative associations. Thao Thao, a journalist for the newspaper *Việt Báo* (Việt News) who visited the Dispensary on the same day as Phụng, commented in his *reportage* about prostitution and the Dispensary, "*Lục-sì* [sic]! What a horrible word!" (1937b, March 3, p. 1). City officials sought to transform people's ideas about the Dispensary by emphasizing its humanitarian programs. Under the guidance of the Prophylactic League, a work room *(ouvroir)* was built at the end of 1935 wherein prostitutes engaged in knitting, embroidery, and other sewing-related activities for the production of garments. Working in conjunction with the Red Cross, the women produced a large number of items that were donated to charity, particularly items for infants. This work routine helped fight the "harmful idleness" that the women had to deal with in the Dispensary while also teaching them a skill that could potentially help them avoid returning to prostitution (Ligue Prophylactique de la Ville de Hanoi 1937, 13). As described in Phụng's text, women also received classes in sexual hygiene and reading. The significance of the latter requires mention because of the extremely high levels of illiteracy in colonial Vietnamese society, notably among women. Joyeux, writing for the Prophylactic League, commented that "nearly all" of the Dispensary women were illiterate when they entered (Ligue Prophylactique de la Ville de Hanoi 1937, 13). Finally, officials sought to emphasize that the Dispensary offered free health care and job training to women who sought it, regardless of whether they worked as prostitutes or not. Given these charitable dimensions, which genuinely were devoted to improving the lives of Hanoi's prostitutes by treating their diseases and providing them a means to leave prostitution, Phụng in the original title and the text alternates between referring to the Dispensary as either Lục Xì or Nhà Lục Xì or the more positive term Nhà Phúc Đường, a generic term for a charitable establishment. As his comments reveal, however, he himself was unsure of which was the more accurate term.

THE SERVICE DES MOEURS AND THE GEOGRAPHY OF COMMERCIAL SEX IN COLONIAL HANOI

The regulatory regime established for prostitution in Hanoi gave the Municipal Dispensary the role of monitoring and treating diseases in the prostitute population through sanitary visits by registered prostitutes who worked in licensed brothels. Records from the city's Bureau of Hygiene indicate that in most years Hanoi had approximately twenty licensed brothels, or "red-numbered" houses (other houses had numbers written in white on blue backgrounds).[11] At the time of writing Lục Xì, Phụng claims that there were sixteen licensed brothels. For the most part, these establishments were located in the old part of the city north of Hoàn Kiếm Lake. Despite their official endorsement, licensed brothels usually did not have large numbers of registered prostitutes working in them. An 1896 police report indicates that there were on average less than 7 prostitutes in the city's sixteen licensed brothels

(MH 2580), while in 1930 the average had increased to only a little under 8 prostitutes in twenty licensed brothels (Joyeux 1930, 459). Data, unfortunately, are not available for the intervening years. In the aggregate, Hanoi also never had large numbers of registered prostitutes. According to data compiled annually by the city's Bureau of Hygiene, they could be counted in the hundreds. The earliest number I was able to locate was for 1908, when there were 120 Vietnamese and 30 Japanese registered prostitutes in Hanoi (RST 71907). These numbers had increased to some 650 by the mid-1920s (see Coppin 1930, 568), but by 1936 Charbonnier (1936, 11) noted the number had declined to approximately 600. These figures, however, concealed a number of problems with the system. According to Cognacq, in 1915 there were over 2,000 women working as prostitutes, but only 137 were registered (6.9%) (MH 2585); then in 1936, when Mayor Edouard Henri Virgitti made the claim that Phụng quotes to begin *Lục Xì,* there were an estimated 5,000 women working as prostitutes, but only 600 were registered (12%). Equally compelling was the number of legal prostitutes who had "taken flight" *(en fuite),* meaning that they no longer reported for their weekly medical examination. Coppin (1930) reported that of the 650 women on the police register in 1925, some 450 (69.2%) no longer reported, and Charbonnier (1936, 11) reported that in 1936 approximately two-thirds did not. The effective regulation of prostitution simply did not work. The commercial sex industry existed largely outside of official control and was dominated by what French officials referred to as "clandestine prostitution" *(prostitution clandestine)* or what the Vietnamese perhaps more accurately referred to as "non-tax-paying" *(lậu thuế)* prostitution.

The existence of this enormous illicit sex trade placed a tremendous burden on a second organization that played an important role in the surveillance and regulation of prostitution, the Service des Moeurs. Similar to the Municipal Dispensary, Hanoi's Service des Moeurs was modeled upon the system employed in France, and as Harsin (1985, xvii) has noted, it drew its name from its responsibilities to protect public "morality" *(moeurs).* Hanoi's 1888 regulations had given the responsibility for the regulation of prostitution to the police commissioner, who in turn was assisted by one "morality agent" *(agent des moeurs)* (Joyeux 1930, 616). Regulations implemented in the spring of 1907 modified this system by transferring responsibilities to the police commission, as opposed to the commissioner alone, as well as by introducing a new Service des Moeurs (Joyeux 1930, 626). Under this system, the police commission was to appoint one or more "inspectors of morality" *(inspecteurs des moeurs)* from within the department's ranks who would be "specially charged" with the policing of the licensed prostitutes (Joyeux 1930, 626). Although it was not officially described in the regulations, the French inspector was assisted by Vietnamese police officers who numbered anywhere from one agent in 1910 (MH 2583) to three to five agents in 1917 (MH 2585) and thereafter. The minor modifications to the service that were carried out in 1915 notwithstanding, this structure was still largely in place at the time of Phụng's writing. In order to avoid confusion, it should be noted that throughout the text Phụng refers to the service with its common vernacular equivalent, Police des Moeurs; thus that term is used in the translation.

The Vietnamese described the Service des Moeurs as the Cảnh Sát Xướng Kỹ, which Phụng in the text renders as the "Customs Police" (Cảnh Sát Phong Tục), but the original Vietnamese rendering is somewhat metaphorical, as "Xướng Kỹ" was the term for a woman who sang for money (Đào Duy Anh 1996, 588), itself a subtle reference to possible links to prostitution. In everyday parlance the men who dealt with the prostitutes were described as the Đội Con Gái or the "Girls' Squad." As the numbers indicated, the service was chronically understaffed, not to mention underfunded. A constant refrain in official and medical circles from the earliest years of the colonial presence through the time of Phụng's writing was that the service was basically a useless and ineffective organization that was completely unprepared to handle the immense realities of prostitution in the city. Although such critiques were accurate, they had little effect, and the officers in the service were still required to carry out the business of policing the commercial sex trade. As Phụng describes in the text, one important responsibility of the inspector was to assist in the management of the sanitary visits at the Dispensary, though the 1907 regulations clearly prohibited him entry to the examination room unless it was requested by the examining doctor (see Joyeux 1930, 626). The primary responsibility of the Service des Moeurs, however, was the everyday surveillance of the sex industry; its staff members therefore patrolled the city's streets at night, often riding around in rickshaws in order to ensure that the city's regulations were being followed.

To appreciate just how unprepared the Service des Moeurs was to fulfill these responsibilities, it is useful to describe the administrative framework within which it worked, as well as the infrastructure of the illegal commercial sex industry. To begin with the former, the Service des Moeurs was part of the Hanoi municipal administration and therefore had jurisdiction only within the city's borders. Vietnam is frequently referred to as a French colony, which is basically an accurate statement as the French did have ultimate authority. Within Vietnam, however, there were distinctions between areas classified as "protectorates," such as Tonkin in the north and Annam in the center, and those classified as "colonies," such as Cochinchina in the south. The important distinction was legal in that in the protectorates, Vietnamese law prevailed, whereas in the colonies, French law prevailed. When the French and the Vietnamese monarchy negotiated the 1884 Patenôtre Treaty, which definitively recognized French control over the north, Tonkin was defined as a protectorate, but the city of Hanoi, which was recognized as the capital of Tonkin and all of Indochina, was classified as what Phụng refers to in his text as "colonial land" *(đất thuộc địa)*. Within Hanoi proper, therefore, the French legal system prevailed, yet once one crossed into the adjacent provinces of Hà Đông or Bắc Ninh, Vietnamese law prevailed. In 1938, Mayor Virgitti and Dr. Joyeux commented that the consequence of such an arrangement was that "the limits of the city of Hanoi are not only municipal, but also and above all veritable national frontiers" (Virgitti and Joyeux 1938, 1). The implications of this system for prostitution were profound because it meant that municipal officials lacked the authority to intervene in prostitution-related matters in the city's outskirts. As described by Phụng in the text, this had the practical consequence of ringing the city with numerous commercial sex establishments and creating a space where sex workers could go without fear of trouble from city officials.

Municipal regulations created another set of difficulties for the officers of the Service des Moeurs in that they were restricted in the locales that they could enter and inspect. From the earliest days of the French presence, authorities had sought to keep prostitution-related activities indoors and off the streets, but this was not formalized until the 1907 regulations that prohibited licensed prostitutes from solicitation in public areas (Joyeux 1930, 622). Despite possessing the authority to keep the streets free from solicitation, agents enjoyed only limited success in doing so. From the earliest years of the French military presence, prostitutes throughout Vietnam would gather after dark in the areas around garrisons. Prostitutes, male and female, gathered outside the Citadel, the primary garrison for French soldiers in Hanoi. This was as true in 1910 as it was in 1930 (MH 2583). Coppin (1930, 570) reported in 1925 that Hanoi's prostitutes had even come up with the innovative method of traveling the city's streets in rickshaws in search of customers. On the streets in which licensed brothels were located, prostitutes sometimes still called out to passersby, to the chagrin of the police.

Agents faced a greater problem with regard to entering and inspecting the sites in which prostitution was conducted. According to city regulations, agents were permitted to inspect only licensed brothels and were forbidden from inspecting any locales in which clandestine prostitution was conducted. Unsurprisingly, the latter vastly outnumbered the legal sites and took a variety of different forms. At the most formal level, clandestine prostitution was conducted in clandestine brothels (*maisons clandestines* in French and *nhà thổ lậu* in Vietnamese). These were situated throughout the city, and although generally of a transient nature, their locations were often known to the agents of the Service des Moeurs, who monitored the sites and submitted reports on their activities. Another location for clandestine prostitution was in licensed brothels. It was relatively common for licensed brothels to have a mixture of women who were registered, "in flight," and unregistered. In some circumstances, the clandestine prostitutes openly worked in the licensed brothel, at least until the Service des Moeurs agents arrived, whereupon, according to the complaints from the agents, they all fled. A more concealed method of operation was for the licensed brothels to have "annexes," which were usually separate buildings within the brothel's compound that clandestine prostitutes or women avoiding their sanitary visits used for their assignations. Charbonnier (1936, 23–24) reported in 1936 that the annexes were usually of the same dismal character as the main buildings. He also noted that many women working in the annexes were registered women in flight and that they were among those most heavily afflicted by venereal diseases.

A variety of other locales, generally referred to as *maisons de rendez-vous* (rendezvous houses), also served as places for clandestine prostitution. Hanoi featured a number of cafes, opium dens, dance halls, and other establishments that sometimes provided settings for meeting prostitutes and in some cases had rooms available for sexual encounters. As Phung shows to great effect, many hotel "boys" (men who worked assisting customers in hotels) would also procure women for guests in their rooms. Perhaps the most infamous location for clandestine prostitution was a type of hotel that the French referred to as the *garni* and the Vietnamese described as the *nhà săm*. The semantics of the *nhà săm* are difficult. At the simplest level it was a hotel, but both the French and the Vietnamese distinguished it from a "real" hotel (*hôtel* or *khách sạn*), which had a more upscale and often more European clientele. Many of these, such as Hanoi's famous Metropôle Hotel, technically prohibited prostitutes on their premises. The *nhà săm* was therefore a type of hotel that catered primarily to the Vietnamese, though mostly those from the lower segments of Vietnamese society. Charbonnier noted that "The patrons are often those of doubtful morals" and that in some cases the *nhà săm* had arrangements with neighboring female venders to provide sexual services to their customers (1936, 24). The most common arrangement was for individuals who had set up an arrangement with a prostitute to repair to the *nhà săm* for their encounter. Charbonnier commented that these were establishments where "comfort and hygiene leave much to be desired" (1936, 24). They also constituted something of a morally dubious space, a point that Phụng supports by repeating Joyeux's comment that a morally upstanding woman would never enter a *nhà săm*. In the text Dr. Adrien Le Roy des Barres also noted that the clientele at the *nhà săm* could pay by the hour or half day. Given all these facts, I have translated *nhà săm* as "seedy hotel."

ABUSE AND THE IMMINENT DANGERS OF THE MUNICIPAL DISPENSARY AND THE SERVICE DES MOEURS

As the discussion above indicates, by the time of *Lục Xì*'s writing, Hanoi's commercial sex industry had grown into a large, multifaceted phenomenon. It not only had a complex infrastructure, but it also engaged thousands of people in a variety of ways, many of them less than savory. In order to begin to understand Phụng's anxieties about the Municipal Dispensary and prostitution in Hanoi, the best starting point is to clarify his thinking about the city of Hanoi as the context for the changes that concerned him. Phụng had been born and raised in Hanoi, and in many of his writings, Hanoi is not simply a backdrop to the narrative but a central character in it. In his fiction and *reportages* he explored the city's darker, seamier, or morally ambiguous sides, as many of the French writers he read, such as de Maupassant, Hugo, and Zola, had done for French cities. Nevertheless, Phụng saw in Hanoi something potentially noble or even grand. As he recognized, Hanoi was an ancient city. It had become the first capital of an independent Vietnamese kingdom in 1010 and had subsequently served, during various periods, as its capital for over five centuries. Beyond this political and administrative importance, the city was also one of Vietnam's preeminent cultural centers, a point Phụng emphasizes throughout the text by repeatedly invoking the vernacular metaphor that described Hanoi as a city of "a thousand-year civilization" *(nghìn năm văn vật)*. Indeed, this metaphor captures for Phụng a sense of the ideal of what the city should be and a standard against which to measure the contemporary city. Unlike the presumed inferiority of Vietnamese society and culture implied in colonial rhetoric, Phụng held that the Vietnamese had historically possessed standards and values of which they could be proud. While cataloging the numerous anxiety-generating problems discussed in the text, Phụng therefore repeatedly asks, "Is this worthy of a city of a 'thousand-year civilization'?"

Against this conceptual backdrop one of Phụng's most immediate and obvious sources of anxiety becomes evident: the possible abuses of women that occurred in the process of arresting them for transfer to the Dispensary, the gynecological exams to which they had to submit, the indeterminacy of their detention, and the sometimes brutal environment that existed within. As noted above, the Police des Moeurs was responsible for policing the commercial sex industry, yet both Phụng and a large number of French doctors agreed that the members of this organization, particularly its Vietnamese agents, were periodically guilty of significant abuses of their authority. Such abuses took the form of demanding bribes, making false arrests, inconsistency regarding who was arrested and who was not (the latter usually resulted from bribery), and, in one disturbing case described in the text, the attempted rape of an underaged girl.[12] The problems with the service, however, ran deeper due to the nebulous and inequitable legal statutes that framed its activities. As Phụng mentions, the service's authority was predicated upon two pieces of legislation passed in 1915 and 1921, the result of which was that a woman accused of prostitution was responsible for providing exculpatory evidence, a task that would be difficult indeed, especially given the illiteracy and lack of education of most prostitutes. The combination of abusive officers and an insufficient legal system created for Phụng such a lack of faith in the service that he concluded in the text, "The abuse of authority for dishonest advantage or the proper execution of one's responsibilities becomes an issue of individual conscience." Archival records indicate that abuses did occur, but as indicated in the text, there were also agents who carried out their duties appropriately.

Another source of concern emerged once women were inside the Dispensary's walls. Hanoi residents regarded the Dispensary as a terrifying place. Located in the city center, it was a secretive structure to which access was severely restricted, a point that helps explain Phụng's elation when he is granted access. It was also not a facility into which passersby could surreptitiously get a glimpse. Its front door was guarded, its windows were shuttered, and it was surrounded by high walls. These features accentuated what many regarded as its prison-like character. Inside one of the most difficult procedures to which women had to submit was the medical examination. It is important to note that the Western science of gynecology did not exist in Vietnam prior to its introduction in the colonial period. The gynecological examination was primarily a clinical examination in which a woman had to lie on her back and fully expose her genitalia for inspection by the medical staff, but its most difficult aspect was the use of the speculum, referred to in

Vietnamese as the "duck's bill" *(mỏ vịt)*, which was inserted inside the woman's vagina to check for lesions or other signs of infection. This procedure was a tremendous challenge to the moral expectations regarding modesty and the privacy of a woman's body. Dr. Piquemal, in a 1927 summary of the work of other doctors, tellingly stated of their work, "They note the elevated numbers of registered women in flight due to the revulsion that the sanitary measures inspire in them" (RST 78701). Joyeux, from a 1930s perspective, reiterates in the text women's revulsion toward the procedure, particularly because it violated their sense of modesty. Phụng makes it clear that the speculum's usage was troubling to him, the men who knew about it, and the women who were probed by it.

An examination that turned up problematic results and the subsequent order for a woman to remain in the Dispensary generated a new set of troubles. Detention had the obvious issues Phụng discusses, such as loss of income and possible separation from loved ones, but an added concern was the indeterminacy regarding the ultimate date of release. It is important to note that the most common sexually transmitted diseases from which prostitutes in Hanoi suffered, notably syphilis and gonorrhea, are bacterial infections that are readily treatable with modern antibiotics, but these pharmaceuticals were not available in 1937. As will be discussed below, the Dispensary medical staff therefore relied upon a variety of drugs of inferior effectiveness that produced inconsistent results, and some, such as the 914 that Phụng mentions in the text, were painful and sometimes even dangerous. Thus, women were sometimes held until they were asymptomatic, rather than actually cured, and the amount of time for treatment was completely unpredictable. No known records exist regarding women who were held and promptly released, but various cases indicate that some women were held for months or even years. An 1890 report on the Dispensary noted that in March of that year, a woman named Nguyen Thị Tu [*sic*] had already been held at the Dispensary for over two years (MH 2575). In later years, Coppin (1930, 579) reported the case of a woman who was held for one year to treat her gonorrhea. Piquemal noted in 1927 that it was not rare for a woman to remain five to six months for treatment (RST 78701). Phụng also mentions the case of the prostitute he interviews who was held for six months while another was held for three months. Prior to the reforms mentioned in the text that allowed some women out for the Lunar New Year celebrations (Tết Nguyên Đán), women were not allowed to leave the Dispensary under any circumstances while recovering; thus it is easy to understand why the Dispensary's regime was held by many to be similar to imprisonment, though with no clearly designated sentence.

Apart from a woman's being held against her will, with no recourse to leave, life inside the Dispensary could also be difficult or even brutal. At the simplest level, Dispensary life was highly regulated. Evidence does not exist regarding the extent of implementation, but internal regulations dictated that a woman's day inside the Dispensary was to begin at 6:00 a.m. During the day a variety of activities ensued, such as work, cleaning, medical care, or education, and then lights were to go out at 8:00 p.m.[13] Such common diversions as gambling and opium smoking were forbidden; thus life inside the Dispensary was quite spartan, though the 1936 reforms attempted to make it less so. Another difficult dimension of Dispensary life, which at times drifted into brutality, was the relationship between the women and some of the staff members, notably the guards or supervisors. Dispensary women periodically submitted complaints to the city administration regarding staff behavior, such as a series of extortion complaints lodged against a Dispensary guardian in 1913 (MH 2584). One of the most spectacular cases involved Margeurite Frass, who worked as the chief supervisor from January 1932 until January 1935 (MH 824).

Frass's tenure at the Dispensary began well, but in February 1933, the mayor's office began receiving a series of complaints about her behavior. She was fired in 1935 for violating her contract, and a subsequent investigation revealed numerous cases of bribery, extortion, and brutality, as well as the seizure of the son of a prostitute who gave birth in the Dispensary (the child was returned to his mother after Frass's termination). One agent involved in the investigation commented that the women had "an intense fear of Madame Frass," while another concluded, "The women undergoing treatment in the Dispensary, as well as the proprietors [of the licensed brothels] literally lived in terror of this authoritarian woman who spared no blows" (MH 824).

Frass's behavior was likely an extreme case as there is no evidence of other supervisors being fired, though there were complaint letters about other staff. It is unclear how much Phụng knew about the behavior of other Dispensary employees and the existence or extent of internal abuses. However, his comments indicate that he was aware that staff behavior generated a certain amount of fear among patients. What Phụng was well aware of, and what he describes in detail in the text, were the sometimes brutal dynamics among Dispensary patients. As he graphically describes with the case of a woman who had worked for many years as a prostitute both legally and illegally, significant tensions existed between the licensed and clandestine prostitutes within the Dispensary. Such tensions sometimes erupted into open violence after the lights went out and in fact became so bad that a grate was installed to separate the two populations. Even after the grate's installation, however, registered prostitutes continued to issue threats and put tremendous pressure on clandestine prostitutes to register and join their brothels. When we look at the situation in the aggregate, a visible level of anxiety runs throughout Phụng's text relating to the following question: if the Dispensary was indeed a humanitarian institution devoted to improving the lives and health of Hanoi's prostitutes, why were so many abuses and inhumane activities associated with it?

FILTH, MORAL FAILURE, AND THE SEX INDUSTRY

Given the Dispensary's periodic abuses and inhumanity, Phụng reflects in the text upon whether it is appropriate for a city of a "thousand-year civilization" to have such an establishment within its borders and whether its existence reflects Vietnam's "progress" under French colonial rule. The Dispensary, however, was but one part in the total infrastructure of Hanoi's commercial sex industry, and Phụng was equally concerned about other parts. To understand this point, it is worth describing the physical characteristics of the brothel world. When the French first arrived in Hanoi, prostitution was usually conducted in thatch buildings, referred to in French as *paillottes*. The scholar and educator Gustave Dumoutier complained in an 1893 letter to the mayor's office that five or six such buildings served as brothels near the Direction de l'Enseignment (Teaching Directorate), where he worked. He described them as "squalid" (MH 2576). An 1896 police report on licensed brothels in Hanoi points to the continued presence of *paillottes,* though brick structures had also come into existence (MH 2580). Over time, the trend would be more toward brick structures, though *paillottes* in some outlying areas never completely disappeared. Regardless of what their construction, licensed brothels were regularly condemned for their lack of cleanliness. Dumoutier spoke of the "squalid *paillottes,*" while the officer in the 1896 report noted that some were "repugnant and poorly kept" while others were in "a dilapidated state" (MH 2580). Another officer in 1915 commented on the "repulsive dirtiness" of one licensed brothel (MH 2585). Joyeux (1930, 479) cautiously wrote, "It is preferable to not speak of the cleanliness of these dumps." He thought that the European clients, both civil and military, often preferred to take women away from these establishments because they were "disgusted . . . by their dirtiness, their overcrowding, and their lack of comfort" (481). His comment on the "overcrowding," or *promiscuité,* derived from the fact that the standard setup within the licensed brothels was not for customers and clients to go off to private rooms for their assignations. Instead, the brothels usually had open rooms with bamboo lattice partitions *(phen)* that created what Joyeux referred to as *"boxes d'amour"* (love boxes) (1930, 479) in which the encounters took place. Such spaces obviously afforded little privacy. As Charbonnier noted, the clandestine annexes in the licensed brothels were usually of the same dismal character as the main building, though other places for clandestine prostitution were "very variable from the point of view of comfort and hygiene" (1936, 23–24). Wealthier clients could afford to have assignations in nice hotels, whereas those of lesser means had to make do with less salubrious conditions. Regardless of their level of filth, for Phụng all of these spaces had a morally suspect character.

Another troubling dimension was the sex industry's sheer scale. At the time of Phụng's writing, Hanoi had some sixteen licensed brothels, most of which had clandestine annexes. There were approximately sixty "seedy hotels," the number of which apparently was continuing to grow (Charbonnier 1936, 24). There were the various rendezvous houses, such as opium dens and cafes, that had rooms that could be used for prostitution. There were also various secluded public spaces where trysts occurred. Once one crossed the city's borders into the "suburban zone" *(zone suburbaine* or *ngoại ô),* a startling number of establishments could also be found, particularly in such areas as Khâm Thiên, Bạch Mai, Ngã Tư Sở, Vĩnh Hồ, and Gia Lâm, each of which sat directly on the city's boundaries. According to figures compiled by Virgitti and Joyeux in 1937, there were 6 dance halls, whose "taxi-girls" sometimes worked as prostitutes, 8 seedy hotels, and approximately 250 "singers' houses" *(maisons chanteuses)* in the suburban zone (Virgitti and Joyeux 1938, 26ff.). By the late 1930s, the latter establishments, known in Vietnamese as *"cô đầu* nests" *(ổ cô đầu),* had become the primary locales for prostitution in the suburbs. Historically, these houses had featured a stylized form of singing known as *ả đào,* and the women who performed it were referred to as either *cô đầu* or *ả đào.* The singers played a castanet-type instrument and were accompanied by a type of woodwind and a drum. In the precolonial period, *ả đào* singing had a sophisticated style that required the mastery of linguistically complex texts that were usually poems written in Sino-Vietnamese. *Ả đào* singers sang in a variety of venues, such as during temple rites and in competitions, but they were renowned for their performances for educated men. Similar in a way to the *geisha* tradition in Japan, *ả đào* singing provided a type of high-status literate entertainment for Vietnam's male elite.

Ả đào houses were present within the city limits prior to 1930, but the explosion in their growth in the suburban zone occurred during the 1930s, with the houses of Khâm Thiên Street among the most well known. The diffusion of these houses, however, was not accompanied by a corresponding expansion of the singers' professional training. Many French officials, such as Virgitti and Joyeux, felt that the women who worked in the *ả đào* houses lacked any professional skills and that the houses were little more than glorified brothels. The houses' clientele had also changed significantly as they had moved away from being the exclusive domain of the literate elite and had become "democratized" to include clerical workers, men engaged in commerce, students returned from France, and even European clients (Virgitti and Joyeux 1938, 6). Performance remained an important part of the experience, but in most houses commercial sexual encounters were also an expected feature.

In the aggregate, one can therefore argue that at the time of *Lục Xì*'s writing there were approximately 400 establishments in the greater Hanoi area that in some form or other had links to the commercial sex trade. As Virgitti comments in the beginning of the text, there were an estimated 5,000 women working as prostitutes in Hanoi, while Virgitti and Joyeux (1938, 27) concluded that there were some 1,500–2,000 women working in the sex industry in Hanoi's suburban zone. In addition, there were thousands of male clients who purchased the women's services. For a city of some 180,000 people, sex was obviously very big business.

Phụng was aware of the scale of this industry, and its enormity and seediness were indeed troubling to him. As he notes in the beginning of the text, it entailed a large number of women who worked as prostitutes and spread diseases. Moreover, there were thousands of others—from the madams to the hotel boys to the city administration and ultimately to the clients—who either engaged with, depended upon, or profited from this vast industry. In acknowledging these troubling facts, however, Phụng develops an interesting and subtle argument about the ways in which moral failure was an engine for both the maintenance and growth of this infrastructure. The argument has its obvious dimensions, such as Phụng's condemnation of those, both male and female, who thoughtlessly transmitted venereal diseases or those who preyed upon the vulnerable to lure them into the sex trade. It also has its surprising dimensions—for example, in the text Phụng never articulates the expected argument that commercial sex is by definition immoral and therefore should be eliminated. On this point his position was obviously influenced by some of his French interlocutors, who held that there would always be a commercial sex industry, and thus the important question was how to limit its deleterious consequences. Instead, his argument centers on the recognition that the sex industry at its most profound level represented a society in which too many people had lost the ability to restrain their desires. A useful way to understand this position is through his usage of the Vietnamese terms *ham* and *ham muốn*. These terms imply such obvious glosses as a fondness or desire for something, but at a deeper level they imply a strong desire, the satisfaction of which has the danger of escaping conventional moral boundaries into either amoral or immoral behavior. In the text, this overwhelming desire is focused primarily on three main targets: prestige objects, money, and romantic love.

To begin with the prestige objects, in *Lam Đĩ* Phụng demonstrated a pronounced suspicion of materialism. To his mind, one of the negative consequences of Vietnam's colonial encounter with France was a burgeoning devotion to material objects and the status competition it involved. In *Làm Đĩ*, the heroine, Huyền, on a number of occasions speaks of her overwhelming desire to possess various prestige items, especially trendy fashion items and jewelry, which Phụng linked to her descent into prostitution. In *Lục Xì*, Phụng identifies a similar covetousness in contemporary Hanoi society, notably among prostitutes, some of whom he unflatteringly describes as overly desirous of the latest fashions, jewelry, makeup, or hairstyles. In constructing his text, Phụng also chose to invoke the argument earlier made by Dr. Coppin that the desire for status objects, notably jewelry, in some cases provided the impetus for some women to work as occasional prostitutes. As Phụng describes, there was a great deal of variation in the female prostitute population, with some working full time and others only periodically. In the latter case, women would turn to prostitution as a way to make quick money to pay off a debt or solve some other financial problem, but there were apparently others, particularly upper- or middle-class women married to men with small salaries, who worked periodically as prostitutes in order to pay off gambling debts or finance the purchase of prestige objects, especially jewelry. While sitting in the Dispensary, Phụng openly declares to the supervisor, "Madam, I tremble for all of the 'romantic' women who today are enamored of those modern things, yet in the future they will end up sitting in here." She responds, "That's it! That is the vicious circle. That is . . . what do you call it? . . . The cost of progress!"

The unrestrained desire for material objects was one of Phụng's concerns, but the desire for money brought out a second moral failing of the commercial sex industry because it often engendered duplicity or outright dishonesty. As Phụng describes it, very little in or associated with the sex trade was what it pretended to be. The women working in the trade employed numerous deceptions. These included the false words a prostitute spoke to clients to gain their business or perhaps find a husband, the dissimulation that she was a skilled musician or entertainer when she had no such skills, the elaborate dress and makeup that concealed a less savory reality beneath, the bogus protestations to the agents of the Police des Moeurs, the equivocations of the madams who ran the brothels, and the elaborate ruses used to conceal the symptoms of venereal disease in order to pass the sanitary visit. The men involved in the trade were no better. Phụng directly criticizes the men who, with sweet though false words, lured vulnerable young women into prostitution. His most critical gaze was reserved for the hotel boys. These men, of which there were apparently many, would approach guests in the hotels and then offer to find them a prostitute of their liking. In Phụng's account of the evening he spent with two prostitutes in a seedy hotel room, the boys would demand money for a rickshaw to go pick up the "proper" girl, when in fact they would never leave the hotel. They would instead go relax and have a smoke and then bring in a woman already waiting in the hotel. If they felt they had not initially received enough money for the rickshaw, they would then "testily" demand more. The guest would have chosen from a series of different types of women described by the boys, such as "modern" women from reputable families or virgin girls recently in from the countryside. All of the women would be described as "certain" *(chắc chắn),* a vernacular expression for being free of venereal disease. Whatever the case, the hotel boys' descriptions were lies or deceptions designed to increase their take, thus adding another layer to the deceit that permeated the industry.

The final type of unconstrained desire leading to moral failure that features in Phụng's writing is evident in two descriptors he frequently employed: "corrupt" *(hư* or *hư hỏng)* and "depraved" or "debauched" *(trụy lạc).* These terms, it should be noted, were commonly used to describe people in the sex trade, especially women. The first installment of Thao Thao's serialized *reportage* that appeared in *Việt Báo* just after Phụng's was entitled *Gái Lục Sì* (Dispensary Girls), while all later installments were given the name *Gái Trụy Lạc* (Depraved Girls) (see Thao Thao 1937).[14] For Phụng, the sex industry by definition involved corruption, depravity, and debauchery. However, Phụng's usages of these terms have subtleties that merit further explication. Contemporary Vietnamese morality placed strong restrictions on female sexuality. Premarital and extramarital sex for women were condemned, and even widows were expected to remain "faithful" *(chung thủy)* to their deceased husbands and never remarry. Moreover, in the prerevolutionary period, virtually all marriages were arranged (see Malarney 2002, 149); thus men and women had to submit to the choices made by their parents. This practice meant that there was no historical tradition of morally acceptable open courtship, and although there were notions similar to what can be described as "true love"— an idea best exemplified in *The Tale of Kiều*—the overriding expectations were that women were not to court; they were to submit to their parents' demands, marry the individual the parents had chosen, and remain with him until death, regardless of personal feelings.

By the late 1930s, particularly in a large urban center such as Hanoi, Vietnam's encounter with French colonial rule had led to a profound loosening of these strictures, a trend that Phụng, in line with the comments of several French observers, relates to the weakening of the father's authority in the Vietnamese family. As a result of this weakening, young, unmarried women were allowed to circulate more freely in social life, so they came into contact with greater numbers of men. The danger here from Phụng's perspective was that by this time Vietnam's encounter with French culture had made many people, especially young women, "romantic" *(lãng mạn)*. The central element in Phụng's usage of the term was that "romantic" embraced the idea of romantic love, notably as exemplified in French literature. For Phụng, becoming "romantic" was dangerous as it created an overwhelming desire within an individual to be with another person, and the strength of this desire impaired a person's judgment and greatly increased the likelihood of making a bad decision that could have damaging consequences. Being "romantic" prevented people from duly considering the potential consequences of the choices they were making, cultivated a dismissiveness toward the moral expectations incumbent upon them, and made the fulfillment of the strongly felt desire the paramount consideration. It was particularly dangerous for women as it made them susceptible to bad choices regarding men that could severely damage their moral standing, destroy their relations with family members, render them unmarriable, lead to pregnancy outside of wedlock, infect them with a venereal disease, or (as in the case of *Làm Đĩ* and *Lục Xì*) put them on a path that led to prostitution. In Phụng's thinking, therefore, colonial social conditions had opened up a space in which women could become "romantic" and *act* on it, and this transition had created an environment in which women, due to the poorly considered choices they made, could more readily slide into the moral failure of becoming "corrupt" or "depraved."

Phụng, in his treatment of individuals' "becoming romantic," is obviously critical of it, but there is an interesting nuance in his usage related to the question of agency. Women who became romantic and then descended into depravity had some measure of personal responsibility for their choices, but society was also responsible because it tolerated the changes that had created the social opportunities for women to both experience and act upon these desires. More significant, Phụng repeatedly asserts that men also held an important measure of responsibility. The weakened father bore some responsibility, but as Phụng emphasizes throughout both *Làm Đĩ* and *Lục Xì,* it was men, usually of a disreputable or predatory variety, who created the conditions for women to go down the path to ruin. Throughout these two texts one finds a variety of male characters—hotel boys, rickshaw drivers, soldiers, errant husbands, wealthy young cads on the prowl, corrupt police officers, and others—who maltreat women, often by taking advantage of their trust, poverty, and/or credulity. And, of course, there was no shortage of male clients from all levels of Vietnamese society who used women and kept them in lives of corruption and depravity. Thus while the descent into corruption and prostitution was indeed a type of moral failure for women, this failure was not confined to them alone, as it was the army of male enablers who often pulled them into the sex industry and kept them there. As Phụng argues in his critique of those he calls "misguided moralists" *(bọn đạo đức "không phải đường"),* who singled out women as morally corrupt, the moral failures of the commercial sex industry belonged to both women and men.

POVERTY AND PROSTITUTION IN COLONIAL HANOI

The anxieties Phụng articulates with regard to the deleterious consequences that emerged in the colonial period due to the loosening of restraints on desire all demonstrate that for Phụng such changes could not be regarded as progress. His engagement with this issue, however, while obviously critical, was related to a deeper question: why did women become prostitutes? The recruitment question featured prominently in *Làm Đĩ,* and in the initial pages of *Lục Xì* Phụng reengages the issue when he raises the question of whether most of the women who become prostitutes do so because they enjoy it. In the early sections of the text Phụng seems intrigued by this argument, which places the blame squarely on the women involved, and his discussion of the avariciousness of some of the occasional prostitutes in earlier sections fits with this argument as well. However, an interesting point that emerges in the text, likely due to the fact that *Lục Xì* was written and published in serialized form over a three-month period, is that Phụng's personal experiences appear to have served as a corrective, and as the text progresses, he moves away from this initial argument and advocates another that places the responsibility for resorting to prostitution more squarely upon the socioeconomic realities that many women faced in colonial Vietnam.

To appreciate this point, it will be useful to provide more detail on the characteristics of prostitutes, which Phụng and his readers understood but about which he provides limited information in the text. Systematic evidence on such points as the average age of prostitutes or their places of origin over time does not exist, though archival records and other sources give some helpful glimpses. One of the most complete sources regarding age is a 1914 list compiled by the Service des Moeurs of the women held in the Municipal Dispensary on the evening of February 17–18, 1914. Of the thirty-one women, one was 45, four were in their thirties (with the oldest 38), one was 29, another was 28, and the remaining twenty-four (77.4%) were aged 18–24. The average age of the last group was 20.2 years (MH 2584). Other documents in the same file and others show a preponderance of women in the 18–20–year range, though older women were involved as well. One particularly sad case was that of Nguyễn Thị Xuân, a 35-year-old from Thái Bình Province who, according to a 1916 report, had been hospitalized eight times for venereal disease. She had apparently left home at the age of 9 and was considered no longer fit for prostitution (MH 2584). Equally shocking were the cases of Nguyễn Thị Lai, 16 years of age, and her friend Nguyễn Thị Nhu, 14, both of whom were treated in the Dispensary in 1913. Nhu, in fact, was treated for several months (MH 2584). Joyeux (1930, 460) noted that many women started working as prostitutes at 12 or 13. Women were supposed to be 18 to register as prostitutes, but younger women obviously entered the trade, a trend likely influenced by the clients' preference for virgins in order to avoid infection with a venereal disease. Coppin (1930, 570) claimed in 1925 that the immense majority of prostitutes were older, though he never provided any numbers, and his comments appear to apply only to licensed brothels and registered prostitutes. Joyeux in 1930 said the majority were between 18 and 30, and later Charbonnier commented that almost all prostitutes were in the 18–35–year range. He interestingly noted that the economic crises of the 1930s had brought many younger women into prostitution (1936, 13).

The most comprehensive source for place of origin is again the 1914 list. Of those thirty-one women, nine came from Hà Đông Province (which was adjacent to Hanoi on the east and southeast side) and seven came from Hanoi, while others came from the city of Haiphong (two), and such Red River delta provinces as Nam Định (five), Hà Nam (two), Thái Bình (two), Hưng Yên (two), Phủ Lý (one), and Kiến An (one) (MH 2584). In other words, 71% of the women came from rural areas, a figure that, based upon scattered evidence in other files, probably underrepresents the rural origins of most prostitutes, though that is conjecture. In the text Phụng makes a number of references to the putative places of origin of different prostitutes, all of which are in the countryside.

The predominance of rural areas as the places of origin points to both the primary cause for entry into prostitution and another source of Phụng's anxieties regarding prostitution and venereal disease: poverty. It was true, as Phụng acknowledged, that various paths into prostitution existed—notably for the occasional prostitutes who worked only for immediate gains—but for the majority, prostitution represented the most compelling, if not the only, solution to poverty.[15] Dr. Eugène Guillemet commented that the "frequent destitution" of local women made it easy for them to enter prostitution (quoted in Abadie-Bayro 1930, 552). According to Joyeux (1930, 460), most clandestine prostitutes came from poverty. Charbonnier perhaps summed this situation up best. When arguing for the introduction of a policy to warn off those who had just started to work as prostitutes, he countered his own argument by noting that "It can thus be said that the depraved are not very numerous; many among them have gone into prostitution because of poverty and the lack of work" (1936, 61).

The poverty of prostitutes was readily visible. Phụng comments on the ragged and threadbare clothing that many of them wore. Thao Thao described the prostitutes he encountered in the Dispensary as "coarse, dirty, languid" (February 16, 1937, 1). Culturally constructed ideas of filth were associated with prostitutes, and the need to eliminate its various forms was perhaps best exemplified in the slogan painted on the wall of the Dispensary's classroom: "Nobody loves a dirty person" (Chẳng ai yêu người bẩn thỉu). Dirtiness aside, many prostitutes did not look healthy. French physicians confirmed their often poor physical condition, even excluding venereal disease. For example, Guillemet commented in 1915 about the women who loitered around a Hanoi garrison: "There are women there of all ages, dressed in rags that cover up vermin, and who carry on their faces or bodies the evident stigmata of syphilis" (quoted in Abadie-Bayro 1930, 544). Coppin commented of the population of Vietnamese prostitutes in 1925 that "this troop is composed of an immense majority of older women, repugnant and dirty, and very often riven with scabies" (1930, 570). Charbonnier later continued that "In effect, these women are far from being clean, often riven with scabies, because scabies are a rather widespread affliction among the poor class in Tonkin" (1936, 12). (Scabies is a skin infection caused by mites that burrow under the top layers of skin to lay eggs. Apart from causing severe itching, the condition also produces bumps, blisters, or even a hard scaling of the skin. Given that it commonly affects such visible places as the areas between the fingers, wrists, and elbows, it was an easily identifiable symbol of poverty.) Thao Thao (February 17, 1937, 3) noted that prostitutes used makeup to conceal the dark colored marks from scabies. For many prostitutes, their clothes and bodies openly displayed their poverty.

Another measure of the poverty of prostitutes was the fees they charged. Although there existed in the Hanoi prostitute population a few so-called "deluxe hens" *(poules de luxe)* who could charge higher fees, most prostitutes charged very little for their encounters. Charbonnier comments that fees were subject to variation, particularly according to the type of client. A coolie was charged 10–20 sous (1–2 hào), a soldier or laborer 25–30 sous (2.5–3 hào), a Vietnamese noncommissioned officer or European soldier 50 sous (5 hào), and a European 2–3 piasters (20–30 hào) (Charbonnier 1936, 17).[16] It is worth noting that according to various newspaper advertisements in early 1937, it cost 3 sous to purchase one copy of *Việt Báo,* 60 sous for one dose of Thuốc Năm *1935* (a gonorrhea medication, with severe cases apparently requiring two doses), and 20 piasters for a high-quality satin top. The clientele of the prostitution industry was dominated by coolies, laborers, and soldiers; thus for the vast majority of prostitutes, encounters produced very little income. Phụng poignantly describes in the text how women, due to desperation, are forced engage in sex in empty areas in the city for just a few sous.

It is clear that Phụng was deeply troubled that prostitution, which in turn brought its own sources of suffering, was the only possible solution for the poverty and deprivation of many women. Thao Thao echoes this same sentiment in his *reportage* on the Dispensary. He tells the stories of Lan and Tuyết, two women whose poverty drove them into prostitution and ultimately to the Dispensary, where he met them. Lan had been born into a poor family and dreamt of wealth. Although her entry into prostitution is unclear, one day a client took her to a seedy hotel with a promise to pay her five piasters. She fell asleep after their encounter, and the client slipped off with all her clothing and without paying the bill. In a cruel shakedown, Lan had to take out a debt to the hotel proprietress and sell herself to pay off the debt. She was later arrested by a Police des Moeurs officer one evening when leaving the hotel (Thao Thao, February 24, 1937, 2).

Tuyết was also poor. In her mid-twenties in 1937, she had four years before been in love with a young student who was also poor but who received financial support from his relatives in southern Vietnam. A neighbor who was attracted to her decided to destroy their relationship by secretly informing his southern relatives about it. The latter stopped sending money and told the student to return. He abandoned his studies, and the couple for a time was forced to live on cod liver oil and quinine to stave off hunger. He later returned to the south and died not long after. Tuyết had, however, become pregnant and soon gave birth. In a bid to support herself and her child, she became the minor wife of the interested neighbor (which was legal at that time), but his first wife would not stand for it, so Tuyết fled to Hanoi's outskirts. There she set up a stand to sell drinks, but the venture soon failed, and without any means, "she had to listen to the enticing words of the rickshaw drivers" and went into prostitution. She was picked up by the Police des Moeurs, and without anyone to adequately care for it, her child became ill and died (Thao Thao, February 24, 1937, 2).

Phụng tells the stories of two more prostitutes, Lành and Yến, two women of similar backgrounds whose poverty drove them into prostitution. However, Phụng's approach also quietly asserts that while poverty was indeed a significant factor, a more profound issue was the social and economic vulnerability of women, which opened them to sexual exploitation by men. In colonial Vietnam, women had few options available to them to independently earn an income, and those that they did have, such as Tuyết's drink stand or Lành's selling of assorted fruits, often generated little income. Women were structurally vulnerable, particularly if they lacked familial support; thus when their limited options failed, prostitution became one of the only viable options left to them. Phụng also highlights the fact that ultimately it is usually men who take advantage of these vulnerable women and draw them into prostitution. The attention that Phụng gives to Lành's life story demonstrates this position. Lành's path to prostitution begins with her being abandoned as an orphan when she was a young girl. Young, vulnerable, and poor, she is enticed by a Vietnamese soldier into her first commercial sexual encounter. Phụng indicates that there was a certain curiosity for her that led her to agree to the request, but ultimately the choice was about survival. It is significant that it is a man who is ready to exploit her vulnerability and lead her into prostitution.

As noted above, as *Lục Xì* progresses, Phụng changes his tone regarding the issue of why women enter prostitution. In the first chapter, he takes a relatively hard line, in which he asserts that many women enter prostitution not because of need but instead because of an "art for art's sake" mentality in which they do it for pleasure or other morally suspect reasons. However, by the narrative's end he has become much more openly sympathetic to the women. He brings this point powerfully into focus in the description of the evening he spends with Lành and Yến in the seedy hotel. Even though he finds Lành quite repellent, he is very sympathetic to her plight. The inclusion of these women's stories is clearly part of an effort to humanize the women for his readers by describing their suffering and demonstrating male responsibility for prostitution. However, what he excludes here is equally significant. In his *reportage* on the Dispensary, Thao Thao's presentation of the case of Lan is basically sympathetic, but he intimates that she is covetous and materialistic. He takes this point further in his description of a third woman named Sen, who is the wife of a government employee with a limited salary. Apparently most of the women in Sen's circle of friends, Thao Thao asserts, played cards with their neighbors, and Sen turned to occasional clandestine prostitution to cover her gambling debts; she was ultimately caught and sent to the Dispensary. Thao Thao concludes: "Fond of the new, fond of partaking of the 'new, strange' pleasures of men who are not their husbands, thus many women have run from happiness into depravity" (February 24, 1937, 2). In constructing his narrative, Phụng acknowledges that some women were drawn into prostitution for such reasons, but he does not elaborate on any such cases. Instead, the overall point he wants to argue is that because of their poverty, for many women there is no other choice, and that makes them victims.

IGNORANCE AND THE PHYSICAL COSTS OF PROSTITUTION AND VENEREAL DISEASE

By the end of *Lục Xì*, Phụng emphasizes that poverty brought many women into prostitution and that compulsion forced them into lives of suffering and multiple indignities, a point he emphasizes by repeatedly stating that some women had to sell their bodies up to ten times a night. He also emphasizes other dangers prostitutes faced—notably the risk of nonconsensual sex or violence from drunken clients, especially soldiers. Prostitution also presented the women with another form of suffering in the extremely high likelihood that they would become infected with a venereal disease. The existence of these diseases relates to the last of his main anxieties about prostitution because the diseases represented a threat not only to the health of individuals, but to that of the Vietnamese people as a whole. Moreover, the existence of the diseases in part derived from widespread ignorance in the Vietnamese population, a level of ignorance that challenged the notion that Vietnam was in fact progressing. In order to understand this point, an examination of the nature of venereal diseases and their consequences in colonial Hanoi is necessary.

The three main venereal diseases that afflicted Hanoi's population were gonorrhea, syphilis (primary, secondary, and tertiary forms), and soft chancre or chancroids. Venereal lymphogranuloma, also known as Nicholas-Favre disease or climatic buboes, was also present, though on a small scale. It is difficult to make any definitive claims regarding the relative prevalence of the first three diseases because they varied both over time and within the Vietnamese population. Definitive numbers do not exist regarding their relative distribution among the male population, but an analysis of data collected by military doctors between 1914 and 1928 indicates that among the 10,682 cases of these diseases treated among Vietnamese soldiers, 44% were treated for gonorrhea, 35.7% for soft chancre, and 20.3% for syphilis (7.2% primary syphilis, 13.1% secondary and tertiary syphilis) (Joyeux 1930, 471). Military doctors and colonial officials were seriously concerned about venereal diseases because high rates among the soldiery diminished combat effectiveness. Statistics on men from the Venereology Service of the Hôpital Indigène in 1934 listed gonorrhea as the most common disease (39.8%), followed by syphilis (33.4%) (Grenierboley 1935, 53), though these numbers reflect only those who went to the hospital for treatment.

Data on the relative prevalence of the different diseases among the female population are also scarce. According to the 1934 Venereology Service data, 47.1% of women were treated for syphilis and 31.4% for gonorrhea (Grenierboley 1935, 53). With regard to the prostitute population, data are scarce, and the best information was provided by Joyeux in 1930. Based upon a study of registered and unregistered prostitutes at the Dispensary in early 1930, Joyeux calculated that among registered prostitutes, syphilis was the most common (62.5%), followed by soft chancre (26.5%) and gonorrhea (17.5%). Regarding clandestine prostitutes, however, among a group of forty-six who were arrested, 63% tested positive for syphilis, while among another group of fifty clandestine prostitutes, gonorrhea was most common (30%) (Joyeux 1930, 494). Theron, in his capacity as director of the Municipal Hygiene Service, estimated in 1933 that at any given time somewhere between one-third to two-thirds of the prostitutes in the Dispensary tested positive for syphilis (MH 2592). These numbers attest to the variability in infection rates while also seeming to indicate that syphilis afflicted the female population more heavily. Dr. Laurent Gaide and Dr. Campunaud concluded in 1930, citing earlier data from Dr. Le Roy des Barres, that venereal disease morbidity in Tonkin stood at approximately 4–10% for the countryside and 9–16% for

Hanoi, though Le Roy des Barres felt these numbers were below the reality (Gaide and Campunaud 1930, 19ff.). Although a precise figure cannot be extrapolated from the data, Dr. M. Riou noted that in 1936, 6,634 patients visited the Dermato-Venereological Clinic of Hanoi's School of Medicine for venereal disease treatment, a figure that represented 64.5% of all patients. Gonorrhea was the most common disease (61.2%), followed by syphilis (28.3%) and chancroids (10.6%). Riou noted that most of the patients were coolies, "boys," petty traders, and modest employees or functionaries. It is significant that prostitutes only rarely or never came. The 6,634 cases would represent roughly 3.7% of Hanoi's population; thus, considering that these data came from only one medical facility, venereal disease morbidity in Hanoi was likely quite high (Riou 1937, 129–130).

In spite of the deficiencies in the data on relative levels of infection among prostitutes, several points can be confirmed regarding the women's experiences with venereal diseases. To begin with, venereal diseases were a basic fact of life for prostitutes, and avoiding infection at some point was seemingly impossible. Evidence indicates that the overall rate of infection among registered and clandestine prostitutes was extremely high, although estimates vary. Le Roy des Barres (1930, 601, 612) asserted that between 1914 and 1926, 79% of clandestine prostitutes were infected, but that number concealed a disturbing trend in the period from 1921 to 1926, when the average jumped to 91.8%. Joyeux (1930, 495) determined that among 50 clandestine prostitutes examined at the Dispensary, 92% had venereal infections. Charbonnier (1936, 18) reported that approximately 96% of the clandestine prostitutes arrested by the Police des Moeurs were infected, though it is unclear how he arrived at that number. The situation for registered prostitutes was somewhat different. Examining the data for May 20, 1930, Joyeux (1930, 495) noted that 45% of the registered prostitutes had venereal diseases. These numbers, he argued, were a testament to the Dispensary's utility. However, as Joyeux himself recognized, one day's results concealed a more troubling, deeper reality. In a study of 182 registered prostitutes examined in the period between January 1 and June 1, 1930, Joyeux determined that 140 (76.9%) had a minimum of one positive bacteriological or serological exam, while another 35 (19.2%) were hospitalized for chancres or metritis, even though their laboratory tests were negative. That left a mere 3.9% who had managed to remain healthy over a five-month period (Joyeux 1930, 493). What should also be noted, however, is that while the majority of prostitutes suffered from only one infection at a time, some suffered from multiple infections. Concrete data are limited, though Joyeux's data from 1930 had 9% of registered prostitutes with multiple infections and 20% of clandestine prostitutes with multiple infections (494). The difference between the two groups was likely due to the increased medical surveillance of the registered prostitutes.

Given the high morbidity for venereal disease among prostitutes, women were regularly being infected and treated. Theron asserted in 1933 that there were many cases of women who experienced the repetitive cycle of infection, cure, and reinfection (MH 2592). The case of Lành, described by Phụng, as well as scattered archival cases, shows that many women experienced multiple infections over time, and recurrences led to multiple stays in the Dispensary. The highest number of recorded infections I encountered was the case of the woman with eight hospitalizations (mentioned above). Dr. Armand de Raymond asserted that the Vietnamese tended to use indigenous treatments first and turned to Western medical treatments only when the former failed (cited in Joyeux 1930, 467), a point that Riou (1937, 130) repeated, while adding that the failure to adequately treat diseases led to longer periods of contagiousness. Joyeux (1930, 496) provides a complete list of the preferred pharmaceuticals for French doctors, among them the widely used "914" for syphilis. The existence of a different pharmacopeia, however, did not necessarily entail any greater success in eliminating the infections. Syphilis, like soft chancre, could be treated effectively, but against gonorrhea, Theron concluded, "We are defenseless"; he further explained that a "misinformed public believes that the women who leave us are healthy and then get infected" (MH 2592). He also reckoned that at any given moment there were 200–300 women ready to transmit a venereal disease, though it is difficult to evaluate that number (MH 2592). Finally, given the limitations of the treatments, some women who were diagnosed with venereal disease were never cured, a point evident in the requirement that incurables were to be "decarded" (*décarté*) and removed from prostitution (MH 2587).

The main outlines of the data presented above were available to Phụng in the *Bulletin de la Société Médico-Chirurgicale de l'Indochine,* which he consulted and from which he extensively quotes in the text, as well as in the documents that Dr. Joyeux gives him in the text. One can therefore conclude that Phụng was well aware of the real dimensions of the venereal disease problem among the local population. However, in the text Phụng is clearly most troubled about the consequences of this situation and ultimately its causes. Phụng was obviously concerned about the level of suffering that venereal diseases caused for the population. For example, one tragic consequence of the presence of gonorrhea in the population was blindness. Gonorrhea is caused by bacteria that, if exposed to the eyes, can cause blindness through gonococcal conjunctivitis. This disease, if left untreated, can completely destroy the cornea. At particular risk are infected pregnant mothers, who can pass it on to their newborns during childbirth. According to the physician Pierre Keller, whose work Phụng cites and who was the director of Hanoi Ophthalmological Institute in the late 1930s, in 1932 there were approximately 700,000 blind people in Tonkin. He estimated that 84% of them had become blind due to external causes and that most had been blinded by gonococcal infection (Keller 1937, 543). Phụng comments in the text, drawing on Keller's and Joyeux's work, that 70% of all blindness was cause by gonorrhea exposure. Keller (1937, 544) wrote that in 1936 he recorded 242 cases of gonococcal conjunctivitis at his institute and that in 1937 there were 312 cases, 194 of which were adults and 118 children. Given the absence of adequate social services, many blind individuals ended up trying to get by as beggars, street musicians, or even fortune tellers.[17] Another problem related to the inability to adequately treat these diseases, or the fact that some Vietnamese apparently left their diseases untreated after the first symptoms disappeared, which left many people with lifelong chronic pain or disabilities. Le Roy des Barres (1931) also argued that chronic untreated venereal diseases were an important factor in the high rates of genital cancers among the Vietnamese, though I am uncertain whether Phụng read Le Roy des Barres's research on this issue.

Yet another dimension of suffering caused by venereal diseases that concerned Phụng relates to the many innocents whose lives were damaged by infection. In the text Phụng repeatedly condemns men who are infected by prostitutes and then infect their unknowing wives. Children were also innocent victims, usually through infection from the mother, though some apparently were infected by wet nurses as well. As noted, some children became blind due to exposure to gonorrhea, but syphilis had its own negative consequences. Coppin noted in 1925 that syphilis and gastroenteritis were the two most devastating causes of the "horrifying infant mortality" among the indigenous population (1930, 586). Indeed, although the numbers had improved from a staggering 370 deaths per 1,000 live births in 1930, Hanoi's infant mortality rate still stood at 210 per 1,000 live births in 1937 (see Malarney 2006). For those who were infected with syphilis but survived, the consequences were often severe. The 1934 data from the Venereology Service indicate that 42% of the 69 children treated there suffered from hereditary syphilis (Grenierboley 1935, 53), and as Coppin commented, these children could be afflicted with the "grave manifestations" of the disease (1930, 586), a point sadly evident in the severe deformations of faces, hands, feet, and teeth that were recorded in a clinical handbook published for dermatology students in Hanoi in 1943 (Grenierboley and Nguyen Huu Phiem 1943).

Also troubling for Phụng was the fact that both gonorrhea and syphilis contributed to high rates of miscarriages, stillbirths, and infertility. Coppin commented in 1925 that "it is not very rare" to have a woman who had been pregnant twenty times but who had only 2–4 surviving children (1930, 586). Both diseases also caused infertility in men and women, though their rates were unclear (Coppin 1930, 586). The combination of all of these factors created for Phụng a strain of what can be described as racial anxiety that runs throughout the text. He makes regular allusions to the fact that venereal diseases were weakening the "race" *(giống nòi)* and that if they were left unchecked, they would undoubtedly leave the Vietnamese people permanently weakened and unable to develop as a society. Racial anxiety as a result of the deleterious impact of venereal diseases was not unique, a point evident in Vaughan's (1991) writing on syphilis in British African colonies. French doctors and administrators expressed similar concerns, and it is interesting that Phụng clearly embraces the arguments advanced by these men. Coppin had written of the "serious repercussions" of these diseases for the Vietnamese race (1930, 584). He and others had written of the necessity to design and implement effective policies to control venereal disease in Tonkin in order to "preserve the race." In constructing his own argument, Phụng does not distance himself from these colonial health officials but instead openly articulates and endorses their arguments.

Phụng's descriptions in the text demonstrate a keen sense of concern and anxiety over the devastating impact of venereal diseases, both individual and collective. Given the reformist goals of *Lục Xì,* a question is raised regarding what he considers to be the primary cause of this constellation of negative phenomena. As Zinoman has noted, in *Lục Xì* Phụng lists over twenty different causes for the prostitution and venereal disease problems in colonial Hanoi, but he does not provide a definitive ranking that establishes which he regarded as the most compelling (personal communication). Nevertheless, when considering the continued propagation of venereal diseases exclusively, Phụng clearly emphasizes that their spread was due to one significant cause: ignorance. Because Vietnamese were ignorant about such issues as the causes, symptoms, prophylaxis, and treatment of venereal diseases, they continued to spread virtually unchecked throughout Vietnamese society. Ultimately, this ignorance was itself the result of an unacceptable hesitation to speak openly about sexual matters.

If one relied exclusively on French administrative reports and colonial medical literature, one would get the impression that the Vietnamese did not attach a great deal of importance to the physical effects of venereal disease. Joyeux commented that "we know that for all the Annamites, venereal diseases are a normal problem, without great importance, and they treat them most often . . . with contempt" (1930, 466). Phụng's commentary in *Lục Xì* is sympathetic to this line of argument, particularly the "contempt" with which the diseases were treated. People became infected, and that was part of the normal course of life; though the evidence indicates that they did treat them, an infection itself appears not to have prevented many people from continuing to have sexual relations. Coppin (1930, 585) recounts a story related to him by Le Roy des Barres of a family whose unmarried son was infected with syphilis. The family sought to arrange a marriage for him in spite of his infection and apparently successfully did so. Within the commercial sex industry, prostitutes regularly continued to work while infected, and their attempts to conceal their infections during the sanitary visits that Phụng describes in the text demonstrate a willful attempt to continue working when infected. It is also safe to conclude, based upon the high rates of infection within the prostitute population, that many male clients similarly engaged in sexual relations while infected.

Given these facts, it is easy to conclude that there was a high level of disregard for others or perhaps even malevolence among those who had sex while infected. Although in some circumstances that might have been the case, such a conclusion assumes that the individuals involved understood that they could transmit their infection to others during sexual relations. On this point, both French medical officials and Phụng argued that large numbers of people either lacked or had an imperfect understanding of the modes of transmission of different venereal diseases. It is important to note that in the late 1930s, knowledge of germ theory was unevenly distributed in Vietnamese society. The concept of the "germ" *(vi trùng)* started to gain currency in Vietnamese society only in the 1920s, and by 1936, the Hanoi-based doctor Bửu Hiệp published a study entitled *La Médicine Française dans la Vie Annamite* (French Medicine in Annamite Life), in which he argued that local understandings of germ theory were indeed incomplete (Bửu Hiệp 1936, 103). It should be noted, though, that in some cases European understandings were little better, a point Phụng emphasizes in his references to the large numbers of prostitutes with anal venereal infections, the result of the preference of European soldiers to engage in anal intercourse because they thought it reduced their chances of contracting venereal disease.

From Phụng's perspective, therefore, one of the primary reasons for the continued spread of venereal disease was simple ignorance. People did not understand the nature of their infections; thus they inadvertently contracted them and transmitted them to others. This argument had a long history in the French colonial medical literature, as well as in some parts of the Vietnamese intellectual community. Coppin (1930, 590–592) openly argued that ignorance propagated venereal diseases, as did Le Roy des Barres (1930, 609). Among the Vietnamese, beginning in the mid-1920s a series of texts was published in Vietnamese that focused on hygiene. This series included a short-lived journal entitled *Vệ-Sinh Báo* (Hygiene News), which ran from 1926 to 1929 and focused on the germ-based etiologies of common diseases and general hygiene issues; it also included a number of publications exclusively devoted to sexual hygiene for married couples, such as Nguyễn Văn Khai's *Nam Nữ Hôn-Nhân Vệ-Sinh* (Male-Female Marital Hygiene, 1924), a translation of a Chinese text; Nguyễn Di Luân's *Nam Nữ Ái Tình* (Male-Female Love, 1932); Nguyễn An Nhân and Lê Trúc Hiên's *Nam Nữ Bí Mật Chỉ Nam* (Guide to Male-Female Secrets, 1933); and Tô Linh Thảo's *Nam-Nữ Phòng Trung Bí-mật Tân Y Thuật* (New Medical Secrets of Male-Female Sexual Relations, 1933). These volumes were distinctly pronatal and took the position that a healthy body, marriage, pregnancy, and successful childbirth all required a scientific understanding of human biology and sexuality. To that end, all discussed venereal diseases and their spread through sexual relations, while the later volumes gave detailed descriptions of their symptoms, and *Nam Nữ Bí Mật Chỉ Nam* featured images of the bacteria that caused various venereal diseases. The latter volume's author even claimed that possessing this knowledge was part of being "civilized" *(văn minh)* (Nguyễn An Nhân and Lê Trúc Hiên 1933, 13).

All of these texts, as well as the *Bulletin de la Société Médico-Chirurgicale de l'Indochine,* were available in the National Library in Hanoi. Phụng had a library card and may well have consulted them there. One significant piece of supporting evidence for this conjecture is that in his novel *Làm Đĩ,* the main character, Huyền, asserts that one of the primary reasons for the chain of events that led her into prostitution was her ignorance regarding human sexuality. *Làm Đĩ* concludes with the narrator passionately calling for greater sexual education to end ignorance and its terrible consequences. French doctors such as Coppin had also argued for sexual education (Coppin 1930, 592), but an interesting point that indicates Phụng's engagement with his compatriots' work is his condemnation of masturbation throughout *Làm Đĩ* and at the end of *Lục Xì.* All of the above Vietnamese volumes addressed the alleged dangers of masturbation, but Phụng's assertion of masturbation's deleterious physical and mental consequences in *Lục Xì* is seemingly borrowed directly from Nguyễn Di Luân's *Nam Nữ Ái Tình* (1932, 25). Finally, these authors also argued that knowledge of sexual hygiene was vital to strengthening the race.

In *Lục Xì*, Phụng aggressively endorses the acquisition of sexual hygiene knowledge, particularly through the attention he gives to the School of Sexual Prophylaxis (École de Prophylaxie Sexuelle) and "The Ballad of Eros" (Phong Tình Ca Khúc). The establishment of the School of Sexual Prophylaxis was part of the 1936 Dispensary reforms. Situated within the Dispensary compound, its primary goal was to teach prostitutes how to successfully avoid becoming infected with venereal diseases. Phụng gives a full accounting of its staffing and operation, but suffice it to say here that it attempted to achieve these goals through instruction on basic hygienic practices and the symptoms of venereal disease. The school's education had a practical, hands-on component that Phụng witnessed, but its defining component was "The Ballad of Eros," a lengthy poem written by the Dispensary staff that describes venereal disease symptoms and prophylactic methods. In the text, Phụng receives a copy of the poem from Dr. Joyeux, who explains to him that colonial medical officials had decided that the most effective way to get the prostitutes to master such information was to put it in poem form. This was a sagacious observation given the widespread popularity of memorizing and reciting poetry in Vietnamese society. Every woman held in the Dispensary in the late 1930s was required to attend the school's classes, and in order to ensure mastery of the poem's content, a woman could not be released from the Dispensary until she could fully recite the ballad. If faithfully followed, the women undoubtedly would have benefited.

Phụng provided the text of "The Ballad of Eros" in one of the early sections in the serialization of *Lục Xì*, and he cleverly used the somewhat hysterical reactions to its content by some members of contemporary Vietnamese society to underscore his argument that while ignorance was a prime factor in the continued propagation of venereal disease, this ignorance itself derived from the stigmatization and avoidance of frank discussions about sexuality. Phụng criticizes the commonly held notion that these topics were morally suspect, an idea emphasized in the usage of the adjective *bẩn* in the discourse on sexuality. *Bẩn* in its simplest form can be rendered as "dirty," but in the context of sexuality, it captures the English-language connotation of "dirty" as in a "dirty joke." *"Bẩn"* topics were regarded as off limits, and discussion of them was to be avoided. Moreover, the designation of these topics as morally suspect was combined with what Phụng regarded as excessive modesty or shyness, notably on the part of women. Throughout the text Phụng employs a variety of descriptors to connote this shyness, such as *cả thẹn, hổ thẹn,* and *e thẹn.* As he argues, this shyness, and a certain measure of shame that accompanied it, created a hesitance or unwillingness to openly try to understand the nature, causes, and prophylaxis of venereal disease, not to mention human sexuality in general. This reticence could have a devastating impact on families when straying husbands brought diseases home to their wives, but in a rich irony that Phụng captures in his descriptions of the prostitutes' reactions to their lessons in the School of Sexual Prophylaxis, it even engendered a reluctance on the part of prostitutes to learn about the diseases and actively engage their clients in order to avoid contracting the diseases. For Phụng, venereal diseases continued to exact their terrible toll on Vietnamese society because of an ignorance that ultimately derived from widely accepted cultural values. In this respect, therefore, Vietnamese society had yet to progress.

The French historian Alain Corbin commented of nineteenth-century French prostitutes that "The prostitute, in brief, did not write about herself" (1991, 107). There are no letters, journals, or manuscripts written by prostitutes that give us insights into their world, and even on something as basic as how they spoke, Corbin noted, "We know almost nothing of their language" (1991, 107). One of the remarkable contributions of Vũ Trọng Phụng's *Lục Xì* is that it provides a unique glimpse into the lives and experiences of prostitutes in late 1930s Hanoi. As discussed in this introduction, the commercial sex industry was vast and constituted an important part of the city's social reality. It was also a reality, however, that was rooted in poverty and suffering, and Phụng's writing eloquently gives voice and humanity to those whose lives were most bitterly affected by it. It is equally significant that through the articulation of his anxieties related to prostitution and venereal disease, Phụng demonstrated that Vietnamese society was beset with serious problems, and these problems themselves demonstrated that Vietnam's encounter with the allegedly superior French civilization had not brought progress. Instead, social and cultural life in late 1930s Hanoi was marked by the breakdown and collapse of significant components of precolonial life, and this loosening of important sociocultural moorings had left a trail of suffering, degradation, and what Phụng described as "spiritual squalor." From Phụng's perspective, Vietnamese society under colonial rule had become "vile and wretched in the extreme." Prostitution, to use his own metaphor, was indeed a "muddy pool," but by the late 1930s, Vietnam's colonial encounter had made that pool more vile and fetid than ever, and its waters sickened all who came into contact with it.

LỤC XÌ

1

A Blemish on the City

One day, during an interview about venereal disease, Mayor H. Virgitti commented to a correspondent from the newspaper *La Patrie Annamite,* "In the city of Hanoi, there are at a minimum five thousand women supporting themselves through prostitution. Five thousand! Yet how can we know everything about them, especially when the solid morality and good character for which the Annamite woman was formerly renowned have become exceedingly fragile due to the allure of changing customs?"[1]

That is the judgment of a Frenchman, a member of the French elite, a top-level official, on the "progress" of our society. To put it crudely so that it's easy to understand, he is saying that contemporary Vietnamese women have become very corrupted.

Five thousand! The number made me panic. I tried not to believe it. But when the mayor of Hanoi announces that the number of women working as prostitutes in his city—an announcement that gives honor to no one—he gets it from reports written by an office we can trust: the Sûreté.[2]

Five thousand! Yes, approximately five thousand, is that right, Sir? There's nothing to doubt about it anymore because it's been stated by the Sûreté. When it states five thousand, though, you must be aware of that number's limitations: it does not include the *ả đào* singers and the dancing girls outside the city limits!

Now, let's make a simple calculation. The population of Hanoi is 180,000; of that number there are 5,000 people working as prostitutes. That means that for every 35 honest people there is one person whose everyday livelihood depends upon the malicious spreading of the germs that cause venereal diseases. In Paris, according to the Police des Moeurs, there are an estimated 60,000 women working as prostitutes. Hanoi, when you consider all aspects, is roughly one-tenth as "big" as Paris? If we do not know for certain, we can probably conclude that Paris is not more than ten times bigger than Hanoi. But in terms of lust and the number of prostitutes, Hanoi is roughly one-tenth of Paris. Those numbers more than eloquently tell us that we have indeed "progressed" very fast!

As for those five thousand women working as prostitutes, Mayor Virgitti holds that that number excludes those who sell themselves in order to get enough to eat because they don't want to starve to death. So the majority of women work as prostitutes only because they like it. In the "prostitution village," there are those who advocate "art for art's sake!" This problem is not merely a social problem. It's a moral problem too.

◆◆◆

In dealing with the prostitution question, the contemporary world is divided into two camps:

1. The "regulationist" camp *(les réglementaristes)* wants to strictly deal with prostitution by putting the brothel trade under legal regulation *(réglementation de la prostitution)*.
2. The "abolitionist" camp *(les abolitionnistes)* wants to eliminate all laws regulating the trade, which is to say liberate prostitution, so that it can be conducted completely freely, all under the name of "abolition" *(abolitionnisme)*.

The former group takes the position that prostitution gives rise to the venereal disease problem, and as the venereal disease problem is a catastrophe for all of society, it is therefore essential to create laws to regulate it, to control it, in the hopes that regulation will lessen its ill effects on the race. The latter group takes the position that freedom of the individual takes precedence over everything and accepts the proposition that "all sexual acts, even in the form of prostitution, are above all the exercise of the right that everyone has to use or abuse his person."[3] They also hold that regulations are ineffective in preserving the race; that the efforts of the Police des Moeurs are wasted because the dispensaries hold only diseased women while men go free; that the Police des Moeurs, because of bribery, often arrest even the daughters of ordinary families or turn a blind eye to women who have diseases. It is therefore imperative that prostitution be free of control. In this way, they hope and believe, society can be relieved of the many savageries caused by the Police des Moeurs and the dispensaries.

France is among the most advanced nations. Hanoi, the capital of Indochina, follows the regime instituted in France. This means that Hanoi has a set of laws that define prostitution; a number of brothels where women work legally as courtesans; a dispensary that holds women and treats them when they are diseased; and a Police des Moeurs that makes prostitutes working illegally enter the officially licensed brothels and hunts down and arrests those who try to flee.

The Vietnamese have their own crude vocabulary for this world. The licensed brothels *(maisons de tolérance)* are *nhà thổ*, the Dispensary is the Nhà Lục Xì, and the Police des Moeurs is the "Girls' Squad" (Đội Con Gái).

To summarize, we have all of the weapons needed to fight against the Bạch My spirit.[4]

Yet how is it that while we are in this city of "a thousand-year civilization," there is for every thirty-five upstanding people one person working as a prostitute?[5] Why are the responsible officials so unable to "know the face" of these five thousand prostitutes that they are able to spread, to their heart's content, diseases among the people? Why does the Dispensary terrify prostitutes and honest women too?

Developing a clear understanding of these questions is not a pointless exercise for readers, male or female, because a *reportage* on the Dispensary is also an investigation into prostitution.

To summarize in one sentence: if we are genuinely concerned about our society and our race, then we must honestly understand the causes of our fears and anxieties.

To do so, I went to find the director of the Dispensary, Dr. Joyeux.

2

The Muse of the Dispensary Girls

Dr. Joyeux still holds the position of director of the Municipal Hygiene Service.[1] His office is located upstairs in a large building belonging to the mayor's office, the place where all Hanoi residents must go at least once a year when it comes time to pay their head tax. To get up there, you must go past the tax office and the business license office and then go up an ironwood staircase. Turning left, you pass a medical examination room run by the city where the government distributes medicine to the poor free of charge. You then get to a waiting room that has a table with newspapers; a few chairs; a desk for a receptionist, where guests who want to be received by the "Director" must turn in their visiting cards; and a ledger for death certificates.

When I stepped in, the room was full of visitors. There were two Frenchmen, one French woman, one overseas Chinese, and one Vietnamese. All of these people must have been waiting a long time. One person listlessly read a newspaper. Another, with a wooden cane, tapped it against the floor in order to relieve his boredom, but that only increased the aggravation of the others. The woman, holding a leather purse under her arm, walked back and forth out on the verandah. I gave my card to the receptionist and, with nothing else to do, imitated those already waiting. I looked at a newspaper, tapped my fingers on a tabletop, and strolled around on the verandah.

Aggravation, if we can call it a disease, is the kind that's easy to catch. The receptionist also went down to stroll on the verandah like the visitors. When he saw a sporty, ultramodern, lightly gold-colored automobile slowly enter the spacious courtyard below, he happily declared, "Ah! The director is back from the mayor's office!"

All let out a long, happy sigh, as if a heavy load had just been removed from their shoulders. The open green flap on the door was closed again, the closed one opened. The French woman came up and said to me, "You came after me, Sir; I must go in before you!"

"Yes, of course, Madam."

The French woman was admitted. I looked at my watch: 5:15. I was worried, agitated. In a few minutes the office would close, so how much time could Dr. Joyeux give me? And would I have enough time to ask to visit a forbidden place, a place where if you are not a brothel worker, a member of the Sûreté, or a doctor, you can never set foot?

5:30. The French woman still hadn't come out. Outside the secretaries and the nurses, having changed their clothes and washed their hands, all filed out to head home.

◆◆◆

5:45. I am finally asked to come in.

"Doctor, please excuse me for inconveniencing you like this."

"Oh! Oh! Please, Sir, sit down; I certainly don't want to create any antipathy with the press."

Dr. Joyeux offered his hand to me in a very collegial way and pointed to a chair in front of his desk. He wasn't as old as I thought he would be. You could maybe even say that he still looked very young. Tortoiseshell glasses, a chin with a trace of shadow from whiskers that a razor can't reach; if only his cheeks were a little fuller, he would have a vague resemblance to a movie actor: Jim Gérald.[2]

"Doctor, among all of the difficult problems that the government must solve on behalf of the Annamese people, prostitution is currently a significant one....As members of the press, we would like to receive permission to enter the [Municipal] Dispensary in order to write a *reportage* that will let our citizens know how the government has been dealing with venereal diseases.... The chairman of our newspaper, Hà Văn Bính, is a member of the city's Municipal Council, and he has already sent a letter to the mayor about this. But I have come to you now to ask you to listen as I lay out all of the things I want to do so that you can support our request at the mayor's office."[3]

Dr. Joyeux cut me off mid-sentence. "Mr. Virgitti has already spoken to me about the matter. The editor of your newspaper did not want to go only as a journalist, but as a representative of the people as well. Because of that, the government could easily refuse the request without any explanation. But in this case, because the city recently spent a lot of money renovating the Dispensary, it's a good idea to let all of you enter. Moreover, contrary to what many French people think, I...I think that maybe the Annamese press could work together with the government on all of the things that need to be done for the people, with the caveat that all of you as journalists cannot intentionally write falsehoods and make bogus accusations against those in the administration. I will dare to promise you right now that you have a real hope of getting permission to enter the Dispensary when all of our renovations are completed."

I was utterly thrilled. Getting permission to enter the Dispensary was no easy task! From the time when Vietnam first had a newspaper profession, and from the time that journalists first started writing *reportages,* among all those of the generations senior to me and among my colleagues junior to me, how many had wanted to examine the Dispensary's secrets?

"Doctor, exactly what day can I enter?"

"As for that, you will have to wait for the mayor."

"Doctor, at the same time I'd like to ask you why we Annamese call the 'Dispensary' the 'Lục Xì.' Even among journalists we do not understand where that peculiar term comes from."

"Ah! 'Lục Xì' comes from 'Look see,' an English expression. 'Look see' means to check for disease. Among the doctors who ran the Dispensary many years ago, there was a doctor who made a lot of jokes, and he frequently used English when he ought to have been using French. I suspect that's how the expression 'Cái Nhà Lục Xì' became popularized among the Annamese."

He stopped for a moment and then continued.

"You should really try to figure out a way to make the people understand that the Dispensary is not a place where courtesans who have diseases are confined like prisoners, but is instead a place where those who have no money can have their diseases treated, and one does not have to be a prostitute to be treated there. *Lục Xì,* that term creates a bad impression in everyone's mind, and it runs counter to the desires of the compassionate people who founded it. The expression *Lục Xì* creates greater complications for the public hygiene problem, even though the Dispensary is a place you cannot do without, and inside it the government is doing only what is beneficial to the courtesans."

The clock hands ticked and became a straight line that descended like an electrical post. Six o'clock.[4] I quickly said the things that I needed to say:

"Doctor, I wish to know how I can cooperate with the government in a way that is beneficial.... My desire is to write a *reportage* about the Dispensary, venereal disease, prostitution. But I am not a medical doctor, nor am I a director of a dispensary! As such, I need to ask you to help me, to give me some materials...."

Dr. Joyeux immediately stood up and went to search in several cabinets that contained government documents and papers. This took five minutes, but it felt to me like it was going to last a lifetime. I had not imagined that a native journalist would be so well treated. When Dr. Joyeux returned to his desk, I had before me the following texts:

One copy of "Le Péril Vénérien et la Prostitution à Hanoi (État Actuel—Bibliographie—Règlementation).
One copy of "Organisation de l'Hygiène et de la Protection de la Maternité et de l'Enfance Indigène a Hanoi."
One copy of "Projet de Lutte Antivénérienne à Hanoi."
One set of typewritten pages of "Le Péril Vénérien et les Moyens de Lutte."[5]

All of these research documents were written by the same author: Dr. Joyeux.

"Here, all of these materials deal with that difficult problem, the problem of prostitution. Read them, and once you have, you will be both a dispensary director and a medical doctor."

"You have my eternal gratitude. Incidentally, Doctor, please let me know what the opinions of the authorities are with regard to the *à dào* women."

"The singing women spread throughout the city, is that what you mean?"

"Yes. Do the authorities classify them as part of the prostitution trade or not? In my opinion, that group in particular must accept a large responsibility for the present venereal scourge...."

"Of course! If they are not prostitutes, then what else are they? I am not the only one who holds that opinion; other men in my profession do as well, such as Dr. Le Roy des Barres and Dr. Coppin, who long ago categorized them as courtesans."

After speaking, Dr. Joyeux searched in a pile of papers and gave me a letter to look at that had an order for two hundred douche bags. At the bottom of the letter I saw a signature: Nghĩa. Dr. Joyeux asked me, "You must know this well-known *à dào* boss?"

"Yes."

"There it is. If it is not prostitution, then why do people ask me to order for them, from France, that number of douche bags? Can the proof be any clearer?"

"But, Doctor, why are there two hundred?"

"Because the boss is ordering for all of Khâm Thiên Street! The more you buy, the cheaper it is."

"If it is like that, then why don't the *à dào* singers have to get examined at the Dispensary?"

"It's only because the people in the region around Hanoi live on Protectorate land and the city has no rights with respect to King Bảo Đại's people.[6] Because of that, the citizens of Hanoi suffer from all of those singing establishments with bogus names that encircle the city with a ring of venereal disease germs, yet the Municipal Hygiene Service has no way to deal with it because the mayor of Hanoi must respect the treaty that the French supreme commander signed with the Annamese king."

"But that is a political problem, not just a hygiene problem!"

Dr. Joyeux dropped his hands to his sides and let out a long sigh. "Exactly. So Mayor Virgitti and I are now preparing an investigative work on *ả đào* singers and dancing girls, entitled "Le Péril Vénérien dans la Zone Suburbaine de Hanoi," which we will give to the governor general's office so that the governor general can clearly understand the dangers they represent for the people of the city."[7]

The hand of the clock showed 6:15.

I stood up to thank him one more time and bid him farewell.

Dr. Joyeux stopped me for a moment, went back to a book cabinet, and grabbed a printed sheet that he gave to me.

"The materials that I am giving you will be incomplete without this."

I looked at the folded sheet. Printed on it, in blue ink, were the words "The Ballad of Eros" (Phong Tình Ca Khúc). Under a tree and a clear moon, at the side of a flowing stream was a woman with her hair done up, holding a moon-shaped lute, apparently singing a poem about hygiene. I unfolded the paper and found a poem like this:

> Life has eating, drinking, fun, and laughter.
> Carousing, betel, smoking, gambling; isn't that enough?

Dr. Joyeux smiled and explained, "The city just finished printing tens of thousands of sheets like that. The goal: to teach prostitutes about hygiene and how to get examined for diseases. Most courtesans are completely illiterate, so the government had to borrow from the muse so that they could learn it by word of mouth and then remember it. It is for the hygiene of an entire race. It is not something for us to look at and laugh about."[8]

"You have my deepest thanks, Doctor. I hope that if I must come again with questions, you will be as gracious as you were today."

"I hope to see you soon, Mr. Phụng."

The doctor offered me his hand to shake.

◆◆◆

Out on the street it was already dark and the electric lights had come on. The guards at the mayor's office had scowlingly locked the door behind me. I saw a gold-colored car turn on to rue Balny.

Several beautiful couples and young women in gaudy clothes loitered gaily around the banks of Hoàn Kiếm Lake. The time for work had ended. The time for play had begun. And with it the time had come to go to work for venereal disease, for the Bạch My spirit!

Just a little while longer and I will be allowed to enter the Dispensary! Which is to say, dear readers, that in a short while all of you will also get to enter the Dispensary. So please read a few "realistic" verses of "The Ballad of Eros" while you wait.

> Life has eating, drinking, fun, and laughter.
> Carousing, betel, smoking, gambling; isn't that enough?
> When you think of your life, you have great sadness;
> The riches over there, how can you dare hope,
> With beauty and talent, you're still unlucky!
> Venereal diseases are terrible; learn how to prevent them!
> Men, they're terrible, such monsters!
> They pour their amorous venom into us;
> If we don't worry about what lies before us,
> We'll give it to others and surely cause greater harm.
> Dear sisters! You must worry, you must think.
> Keep those diseases away.
> All men want to find a flower;
> Check carefully lest you catch something;
> If you see anyone with a forehead full of red spots,
> If you see anyone with spotted patches,
> Or red patches, or black patches,
> On the hands, on the chest, or on the thighs,
> That is definitely a diseased person.
> You must stay far away from him;
> Don't let him slowly get near you.
> He is dangerous like a tiger!
> Take good care! Don't be reckless with your body.
> It rests in your hands and no one else's.

If you meet a client,[9]
Be pleased to let him pick the flower.
But before everything, you must wash things clean.
As you do with yourself, tell your client he must follow;
White soap, clear water;
There's nothing to worry about washing together.
Deftly engage your client, make his enthusiasm rise;
There's nothing strange about it! That's proof he's a man.
When you are near a client, your face becomes crimson,
Love's burning flame, in red you glow.[10]

3

A Few Statistics and a Little History

We need to consult the elderly in order to be clear about where the Dispensary was in the past. Before 1900, it appears that the government had placed it on Hàng Cân Street. A decision of Governor General Paul Bert stated that "Prostitutes who are shown to have a disease must be arrested and held in the Dispensary until they have recovered from their disease."[1] That was written in 1886, meaning that it came two years after the French government had signed the Protectorate treaty with the Huế court. If we go along Hàng Cân Street today, we cannot find a single trace of the former dispensary. Even the director of the Municipal Hygiene Service, working as a "historian" researching the subject, came up with nothing.

From 1902 onward, we can possibly discover a few things that we need to know. At that time, the Dispensary was in a rather grand building on Hàng Lọng Street, near the Catholic cemetery. Then, as the educational system grew, it had to move in order to make way for a school. In 1918 it was temporarily moved to a...shrine. That's right, a shrine, behind the mayor's office, on the site where the city's Children's Park is now located. After that a sum of money was made available to build a dispensary for courtesans, and after construction on that building was completed in 1926, the city moved the Dispensary to the corner of the street in front of the Hanoi courthouse. This in spite of the anger of nearly all of the judges, who vehemently opposed the move because they didn't want the Spirit of Justice to become a neighbor (choose your neighbors!) to that filth.[2]

It is undeniable that the things that chafe the skin of humanity can create a real mess. They've created complications for who knows how many people. For administrators, for doctors, for members of the Sûreté assigned to the Police des Moeurs or the Girls' Squad, for members of the Municipal Council. A decision is made for a new public building, but the justice people don't like it. The Dispensary was built, but then in its wake came a frightful tempest.

The reader can imagine the animated sessions of the Municipal Council. The municipal and military physicians cry out that the Dispensary should "flourish" because the races, both Annamese and French, must be preserved. Other council members object because for them prostitution is a problem that does not submit to administration. The grimacing mayor worries about the lack of public funds, so taxes must again be raised.... The number of advocates for getting rid of the Dispensary is large, their reasoning is solid, but, as usual, the city still has a dispensary. That dispensary will never satisfy the doctors because regardless of where they are, doctors are enthusiastic, zealous. They want reform, development, an increasing effort to protect public health—which means that they want more public funding.... The people never want to understand anything: they just close their eyes and complain if they have to pay high taxes. "With stomach full and back warm, everyone feels aroused."[3] Dear sirs, it is completely legitimate that we have to pay money for this. A few of the statistics below demonstrate the extent of the damage that prostitution has done to our society!

In 1914, 74 percent of French soldiers in Tonkin had some form of venereal disease.[4]

Dr. Keller, who runs the Hanoi Ophthalmological Hospital, has confirmed for us that 70 percent of those in our population who have lost the use of one eye or have become blind have done so as a result of exposure to the germ that causes gonorrhea.[5]

The director of the Hanoi Hygiene Bureau has also informed us that of the four thousand infants who die right after birth, there are on average approximately one thousand infants who, according to our terms of avoidance, had skin diseases, thrush, were abandoned, were lost, or were hard to care for. According to science, these infants die because their mothers and fathers carry the venom of syphilis or the complications of that disease.[6]

That's how it is.

Still, those figures are confined to the city of Hanoi, to colonial land only. But Hanoi is the capital of Tonkin and Indochina! Doesn't everything that affects our people originate in Hanoi? We should be quiet and listen as Dr. Joyeux explains:

Everyone knows that when a group of people has more interaction with other peoples, be it through trade or invasion, that group will more easily suffer from venereal diseases or other infectious diseases. France, during the time of the European war, received soldiers from nearly all its allies; thus France was heavily exposed to syphilis germs, if we speak only of that disease. During times of peace, everyone is fully aware of the public health situation in crowded ports, where there are many foreigners visiting brothels. Now, if we direct our attention to various historical moments of this country, we will recognize that the conquests, by military or commercial means, of the Chinese, Cham, Khmer, and more recently the Europeans, were more than enough, and bad enough, to make Indochina suffer from a serious venereal disease problem. Furthermore, Chinese medical texts have already discussed at length such events as premature births, early deaths, terrible deformities, and skin diseases; these make us conclude that syphilis has not spared the population, just as the excessive numbers of blind people in this region are evidence that the gonorrhea germ has caused harm. These judgments have been disputed by some contemporary doctors, who hold that venereal diseases have really not been that harmful to the Annamese, a peculiar fact that resulted from the government, which was initially indifferent to the problem, only summarily dealing with it once it was recognized that it really was not all that serious. Given the hereditary cold indifference of the Annamese to the venereal disease problem, their opinion is that it is not that significant, and given the degeneration of the moralities of Confucianism, Buddhism, and Taoism, it is therefore the case that a large number of people easily catch venereal diseases, and more diseases have come in from abroad and spread like an oil stain on a sheet of paper. Moreover, there is another reason that has infinitely increased the damage: to be precise, it is the progress that our young people so eagerly follow. The thirst for study, the temptations of new occupations, have led large numbers of young people to the bustling cities in order to escape family morality. The intoxicating powers of getting rich quick, of enjoying the diversions of a Western city, of being without parental supervision, that, all of that, has been the reason for the loosening of the moral system and has allowed venereal diseases to spread even more rapidly. After getting rich or passing exams in the city and then returning to the village or by being appointed to posts in the countryside, members of this group will perhaps become a large wave that will spread who knows how many germs, particularly since their progressive civilization strongly instructs the people in the countryside to respect them and submit to their influence.[7]

These words are very easy to understand. They clearly explain why people in the countryside today have also become very corrupted, and they also help us clearly understand the situation with prostitution and venereal diseases in the agricultural regions, even when Dr. Joyeux cannot clearly explain to us with precise statistics, percentages, etc.

And so it is that beyond all of the other problems of which people are aware and think should be solved first, there is only prostitution that is harmful to an entire race, so it is more important than everything else and must be solved first.

Long live the Dispensary! It will be here forever, even though the faction that wants to get rid of it has set out the following program:

Abolish:

1. Abolish all regulations constraining prostitution, including:
2. Disband the Girls' Squad because common law regulations are the only applicable laws.
3. Close the Dispensary doors. Prostitutes can choose to treat or not treat their diseases as they see fit, or they can voluntarily go to the Hôpital Indigène as in the case of other diseases.[8]

Create:

4. Open a venereal disease hospital that treats all classes of people in a much more thoughtful manner.
5. Conduct sexual education; teach about venereal disease prophylaxis to both Annamese and French, civilians and soldiers, through schools, conferences, films, leaflets, posters, etc.
6. Eliminate those things that facilitate the venereal disease problem: madams; pimps; the affronts to decency; the assaults on good customs; the things that incite prostitution, drunkenness, gambling....
7. Establish criminal and civil laws to punish those individuals who transmit a venereal disease to another person.
8. Protect young mixed-race and Vietnamese women; reform prostitutes, clubs for soldiers, sports circles.[9]

The head of this [latter] faction is a person that all of us know: Dr. Le Roy des Barres.[10]

But as for you men who have a disease and still recklessly go carousing, fear not! No, the time has not yet come for you to go to jail! Dr. Le Roy des

Barres drew up his program in 1927, but to this day it is still but a pile of worthless papers.

Within the Municipal Council it is not simply that there are those who want to constrain the prostitutes through the Dispensary and those who want to get rid of the Dispensary. There are also those in the middle who want to mediate between the two factions.

Do not "liberate" the prostitution trade so it can carry on freely—that is the cry of the "strict" faction, which continues to say that current laws to control prostitution have been a complete failure. The middle faction also knows that, but it argues that if there have been no results, it is because the earlier controls were not implemented carefully and have yet to be taken far enough. It then requests:

1. A Girls' Squad that has an adequate number of personnel and has greater powers to arrest the five or six thousand prostitutes, in Hanoi alone, who do not pay taxes.
2. The unit will be under the mayor's authority, which is to say that it will be under the direction of the city's police commissioner, not as it is now, under the control of the director of the Sûreté Générale of Tonkin.
3. There must be laws that will allow the unit to enter all drinking establishments, opium dens, and suspicious houses that are "devil's dens" in order to look for clandestine prostitutes.
4. Combine the Dispensary with the Hôpital Indigène to create a place where more patients can be treated; as for the money, one-half will come from the Tonkin budget and the other half from the city's budget.
5. Establish Girls' Squads in all of the provinces to help squad members more readily hunt down prostitutes who have fled from Hanoi and who are freely spreading venereal diseases in the provinces or even in Hanoi's outskirts—lands that are part of the Protectorate where the officers currently have no authority.
6. Force the *à đào* singers on Khâm Thiên Street, Vạn Thái Street, and all other places to submit to the prostitution laws because in reality they are engaged in prostitution.
7. Create a designated quarter *(quartier réservé)* for prostitution. The city can find a spacious piece of land, build several large buildings that meet all hygienic standards, and then rent them out cheaply. At this locale there will be police officers from both the military and the

city to maintain order for both civilians and soldiers. If done this way, city residents will be happy because they will be able to remove all of the brothels from the respectable streets, the madams will be satisfied because they will not have to pay high rents, the courtesans will feel at ease as they will be able to escape the fear of violence from drunken clients, and the police will also find it easier to keep order.

This program has been approved by the majority of the Annamese members of the Municipal Council, especially the provision that forces the *à đào* singers to be examined at the Dispensary, but councilman Sỹ Ký (Hải Phòng) has become renowned for his hostility to it.

Dear Sirs....

Do we approve Dr. Le Roy des Barres's program to liberate prostitution, or do we approve the program to suppress it as just explained?

Are we content to let a few of our very dear sisters in the designated quarter be forced to visit the Dispensary and make the acquaintance of the "duck's bill" *(mỏ vịt)*, or are we content to go to jail or provide monetary compensation to anyone we infect with a venereal disease?

Tyrannize and liberate. It's true, we cannot figure out which camp to stand in. Prostitution. It's a problem that has created misery for doctors, legislators, sociologists, philosophers, all of whose understanding is a thousand times greater than our own.

And it's the same with the government!

So one day, Dr. Le Roy des Barres had to let out a long sigh and say, "If in Tonkin there are laws that regulate the brothel trade, laws that are adapted from those in France, then those laws only have the value of a pile of scattered papers. The officials, the doctors, the police all agree that one cannot import and implement those laws."

A bitter truth: it is doubtful that forcing prostitution to submit to established regulations will be beneficial to society, but it is also doubtful that liberating prostitution in order to reduce the waste of public funds and avoid abuses by those in law enforcement will have no harmful consequences for law-abiding citizens!

So what is it then, this human scourge of prostitution, both historically and today?

4

There Must Be Harm

From the time that humans have lived together as a society, perhaps since antiquity, humanity has been tortured by the scourge of prostitution, like the pain of an infected boil or a cancer. Despite the numerous methods used to eliminate it, it still insistently trails behind in all the history books, and it will certainly never make any concessions. Prostitution is an awful calamity, but if humans did not have it, it would destroy them.

The efforts of the philosophers, the legislators, and the missionaries to eliminate it have all ended in defeat. For centuries, the books of sociologists, the decrees of kings, the papers of legal scholars, the proclamations of Popes have all piled up in a heap around that mountain.

This monster fears nothing, and as the pile of papers grows higher, it still is not buried beneath, but instead stretches up to climb ever higher in order to torment humanity.

Prostitution is one of the immortal problems of every race, and all must find a way to cope with it.

The scourge is linked to human destiny as well, as it crushes our fate through a strange and bitter sadness. Human fate is like that: we do not know what creates us, we do not know why we exist, we do not know how we will die, and the even more pernicious fact is that while we are alive, we suffer from innumerable misfortunes, but we do not know their cause. Among those many wounds, prostitution is one.

In ancient Egypt, Chaldea, Assyria, Phoenicia, prostitution was already devastating. In every ancient Asian city, poor people sold their children into prostitution. In countries with slavery, women were forced to give their bodies to their masters. It was the same with the Greeks and Romans, though especially the Greeks, who by nature were a civilized people. Their aesthetics glorified prostitution and adorned courtesans with poetic charms and extraordinary virtues. The truth was that such famous courtesans as Lais,

Phryne, Sappho, Asnasie, etc. were rare characters, and the heroic army of suffering, miserable prostitutes in other places, when it came to talent and beauty, possessed nothing greater than the ragged prostitutes of our land.[1]

The more we return to the old pages of history, the clearer things become. In the Middle Ages and the Renaissance, the scourge of prostitution in France caused venereal diseases so terrible that all of the neighboring governments had to join forces with the Church to eliminate the diseases by employing such harsh methods as beating, quartering, hanging, public shaming, and the seizure of prostitutes' property. Prostitutes were also forced to live exclusively in brothels, were forbidden from going about on the streets, had to cut their hair short, and also had to wear distinctive clothing. Some of these methods are still practiced in a number of countries today. This is some of the evidence regarding prostitution's persistence, and it is the same everywhere.

But there is one more thing worth noting: all of the governments and royal courts had to unanimously acknowledge that they lacked the power to eliminate prostitution, but even if they could eliminate it, its complete elimination would also be very dangerous. Thus, from long ago until today, the position of the legislators has not exclusively been to eliminate prostitution's most devastating consequences, but primarily to maintain it at a reasonable level because they feared that to wipe it out completely would produce even more dangerous and fearful consequences, so it was best to let it naturally persist.

At this point, we again see another different characteristic of the scourge of prostitution that is extremely strange. We have already reluctantly admitted that it is an immortal problem, that it cannot be avoided, but it is also something that we cannot *not* have. Even though it is a terrible wound on all humanity, if we did not have it, humanity would be unable to stand on its own feet because it would lose its balance. One odd problem is that of the two-faced monster, which is similar to the philosopher Aesop's opinion that the human tongue is both useful and ruinous. One point that is hard to understand about humans is that all of the grand theories about Rights, Power, and Logic do not change things the tiniest bit.

Those are the conclusions of Dr. Bodros regarding this particular cancer, ancient and contemporary, Eastern and Western....

Prostitution is a scourge that must exist.... If we had some terrible and miraculous method to instantly eradicate the foul occupation, like we would smash a hammer into the head of a poisonous snake, then what would happen to the city of Hanoi? Oh! No! Even if we had such a miraculous method, we could not use it. Why?

Nine hundred soldiers would become unsettled if these men—who have no wives—failed to completely follow Freud's theory of sexual abstention and limitation that the French call *refoulement freudien.*[2]

Sixteen modern "madams" would follow behind the *one hundred and eighty-five* young brothel women who would fall into an embarrassing situation when they tried to find a new occupation.

Thirty-seven owners of seedy hotels and over one hundred hotel boys would become unemployed.

Six hundred and thirteen owners of official or unlicensed opium dens would commit suicide.

Five thousand clandestine prostitutes—and this number is just a guess by the responsible authorities—would create turmoil throughout the capital.

The city's coffers would annually face the loss of the approximately 1,388.86 francs in licensing fees collected from the sixteen red-numbered houses, yet that number still excludes the revenues that would be lost from the licensing fees for all of the seedy hotels, dancing halls, and drinking establishments.

The army of the unemployed, which would include the hotel boys, pimps, and rickshaw drivers who work the night, would be terribly affected, and this would lead to truly frightening incidents of theft and burglary.

No, no, and no! Wiping out prostitution would be a dangerous thing.

Or do we follow the program of Dr. Le Roy des Barres?

The government lacks the money to implement the creative components of that program. There isn't enough money to do anything. The city of Hanoi doesn't really liberate the prostitution trade, but it doesn't really strictly control it either. With this scourge, the city of Hanoi perhaps can deal with it only in a cursory fashion.

It's just a formality!

The Hanoi Dispensary can accommodate only two hundred people, despite the fact that some five thousand courtesans must be caught and taken to the Dispensary. Approximately five thousand women work clandestinely, but there is only one French inspector in charge of five or six members of the "Girls' Squad." Those five or six people must identify and check 16 brothels, 15 houses with independent prostitutes, and 377 rooms in the seedy hotels! In one night!

A vaudevillesque police force!

Dr. Joyeux, the director of the Municipal Hygiene Service, had to acknowledge that. We live under a system in which no one takes responsibility. That is one of the troublesome aspects of the system of colonial land and Protectorate land created by the Patenôtre Treaty of 1884.[3] It gave rise to all of these tangled complications, such as the fact that the Phủ Doãn hospital is part of the budget of the Protectorate of Tonkin, while the funds for the colony of Hanoi cover the Dispensary.[4]

Like me, the reader now knows a few facts, a few statistics about the Dispensary that might help us understand what we will find inside. We should regard those statistics as a few secrets to hold in our protective magic pouches. As we live under a law that strictly forbids people—including journalists—from even clandestinely entering such public establishments as mental hospitals, prisons, skeleton production facilities, arms factories, military garrisons, leprosaria, etc., . . . we shall carefully conceal those magic pouches.

Well, we've come to the Dispensary.

Standing in front of its frightful door, we only need say the magic words, "Open sesame!"

5

Strolling inside the Dispensary

The Dispensary door had truly opened.

The door opened easily and created a space wide enough for a good number of people to slip in. Was it due to the magic words from the tale of Ali Baba? No. It was due to a visit to the Dispensary by the labor ambassador Godart of the Popular Front government.[1] But that was many days before.

People had worked hard to prepare, reform, fix, and change everything within the Dispensary, all with the aim of showing Mr. Godart the recent progress of this institution dedicated to eliminating venereal diseases and controlling prostitution. Only after that had anyone started to think about the press. The print journalists—of the gutter variety—really don't want to pester the mayor all the time, particularly if the mayor doesn't understand what the benefit is when he is being pestered. In the past, the masses regarded the Municipal Dispensary as a terrible prison, a place of torments, abuses of power, and cruel acts committed by public officials. For the members of the Hygiene Commission, it was a place of errors and mistakes. But the city had provided a large sum of money to fix a number of things that people had legitimately complained about. After we journalists were invited to come as eyewitnesses, we were to go and spread the good news to the people and the prostitutes. It was the first time in our land that those in power had paid even a tiny bit of attention to the "Fourth Estate."

Today is the twenty-eighth day of the twelfth lunar month, Year of the Rat.[2]

The journalists, two from the newspaper *Việt Báo,* one from the paper *Đông Pháp,* and I, had entered and were waiting in the Dispensary courtyard. The mayor was at that time giving a tour to the wives of several high-ranking officials, such as the wife of Supreme Commander Buhrer. At the same time, several other women had gone to see the rooms inside. The city had called to invite all the newspapermen in Hanoi, but only we four had shown up.

Maybe all the others had returned to their home villages to prepare for Tết.[3] While we were waiting for Dr. Joyeux in the Dispensary courtyard, an assistant physician called to invite people from the newspapers *Trung Bắc* and *Ngày Nay*. A French police officer was extremely surprised to see journalists inside the Dispensary. He smiled and joked to me: "You're all journalists? So for which 'rags'? Go on in, and then go write some more garbage!"

Then Mr. Mas, a Police des Moeurs inspector with a very self-satisfied air, pointed to the lush beds of flowers that bobbed beneath the spring rain drops. The flower beds gave the Dispensary the look of a villa. As he gestured, he asked us, "Have you taken a look at that? Does it look like a prison in here? So why do you still call it a prison?"[4]

Outside, right at the spot where you walk in the door, was a group of about thirteen madams boisterously chatting around the guard. They wore black silk pants, gauzy or satin quilted black jackets; even their shawls were black. The most interesting thing about them was that they were all rather plump. They had come to pick up their "daughters" to go and celebrate Tết because this year the Dispensary had established a special privilege for the women who "had papers." They were allowed to leave the Dispensary to celebrate Tết, even though they were not yet fully cured of their diseases. Seeing their timid attitude, so full of courteousness, so easily frightened, and their serious and proper black clothing, no one would dare to think or imagine that these women practiced such a horrible vocation: proprietress of a brothel. Most of them were rather plain, with no flashy makeup at all, but stately in that all were plump. They had something of the tremendous haughtiness of a mandarin's wife or at a minimum that of the gentlewomen of bourgeois or conservative families, who manifest something of the not-yet-modern generation of our society. Thinking of that makes one want to cry out, "Long live Nguyễn Du!" *One noticed at first glance her pallid skin....*[5] There was really only a little bit of that, but they still had enough to give themselves away as madams, and it is not necessary to note that we will meet them again in the Dispensary courtyard.

Mayor Virgitti, an administrator who, due to his proposed residence taxes, education fees, etc., had the misfortune of being regarded as the mayor with the least sympathy ever for the Vietnamese, was one of the victims of the 1884 Patenôtre Treaty—it's always that treaty! It classified Tonkin's budget as part of the Protectorate budget and then classified the city of Hanoi's budget as part of the colonial budget, meaning that Annam was divided as if it were two almost completely distinct nations. Honestly, unlike others, I think that Mayor Virgitti is a good man, but I'm not at all afraid of being publicly discredited. You should conjure in your minds an image of a high-ranking official, the man who presides over the capital of Tonkin, yet his clothes are very simple. A shirt of one color, pants of another color, an out-of-fashion necktie, shoes that are not polished. His manner and language display a hard-working disposition and a simplicity, while his facial features show a quick-wittedness and amiability that is 100 percent like that of everyday people. It is truly different from other officials, who are usually imperious and happy only when others treat them as esteemed personages.

While we were waiting for Dr. Joyeux, the mayor spoke about the Dispensary, venereal diseases, and prostitution. He spoke of the reasons why the government had invited the press to visit the Dispensary and asked all of the journalists to do something so that the people did not have misunderstandings about the Dispensary, so that prostitutes did not endlessly evade it, and so that they would follow all of the Dispensary rules in order to prevent themselves from committing the offense of spreading venereal diseases among the population. Along with the mayor and us, others participating in the conversation were two Annamese assistant physicians; Mr. Mas, inspector of the Girls' Squad; and one French female nurse, who wore a cap with a red cross on it and who served as the chief supervisor. This place was the office. On the wall was a large blackboard the size of a floor mat, upon which were listed in detail, with clearly arranged green and red paper markers, all of the women from the brothels and the brothels from which they came. The blackboard clearly described the medical conditions of the women, the number of women who suffered from disease, and the number of women who had fled without permission. I noticed that there was one woman who was sixty years old who could no longer sell her body and who was now being cared for at a charity home on Hàng Bột Street. On the other side of the room was a file cabinet that contained the documents for the women who had papers, those who had "torn up" their papers, those who worked clandestinely, etc.... The barometer and timetable of the prostitution industry. A museum of filthy things, of infamies, but the ancient Bạch Mỹ spirit had made it such that all of us who pay taxes must shoulder these expenses. A pot of narcissus placed next to the phone box lets all of the pessimists know that life outside goes on as usual, life with wonderful spring days and life with all of its lying and cheating.

Around 4:00 p.m. Dr. Joyeux arrived, wearing a pair of scholarly white glasses and a pair of smart-looking spats that made him look like a doctor in a movie.

So! Let's go visit the Dispensary!

All photographs are from the 1937 volume, Le Dispensaire Antivénérien Municipal et la Ligue Prophylactique de la Ville de Hanoi.

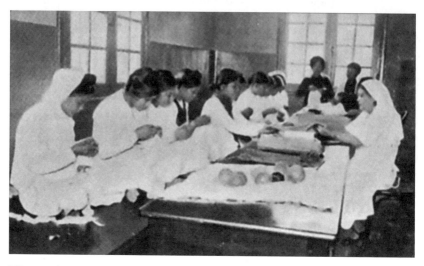

Women learning to sew in order to acquire a skill that could help them support themselves after leaving prostitution.

Here women are being taught to read and write.

A woman is taught sexual hygiene in the "School of Sexual Prophylaxis" (École de Prophylaxie Sexuelle) described by Phụng in chapter 5. Watching the lesson are fellow confined residents. The slogan above the woman reads, "Cleanliness is the best doctor" (Sách sẽ là ông thầy thuốc hay nhất).

A Dispensary employee, perhaps the Nurse Nghĩa mentioned by Phụng in chapter 7, gives a lesson on sexual hygiene. The slogan above her reads, "No one loves a dirty person" (Chẳng ai yêu người bẩn thỉu).

A woman receives a gynecological exam as others wait in line.

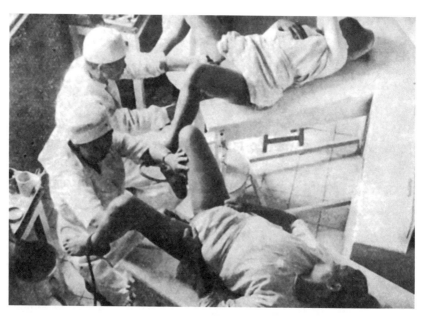

Two women receive simultaneous gynecological exams. A speculum or "duck's bill" (mỏ vịt) is visible on the tray at the top of the picture.

The interior courtyard of the Dispensary, which had been expanded in 1936 to provide a more comfortable recreation space for residents. On the far right is a shrine dedicated to Bạch My, the guardian spirit of prostitution.

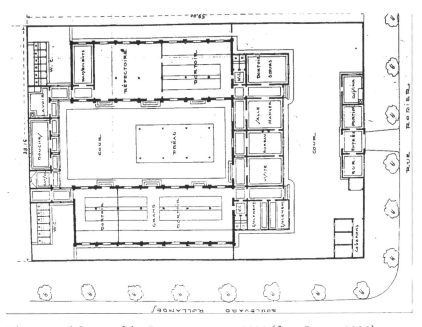

The internal design of the Dispensary, circa 1930 (from Joyeux 1930).

We followed the mayor and the director of the Municipal Hygiene Service. Almost all of the Dispensary workers walked along behind us. Then we turned left.

The examination room. The walls were clean and whitewashed with lime; a zinc table, a spotless white cotton towel, shiny glazed porcelain basins for face washing, cabinets, chairs painted white—it all appeared very hygienic. All of these things were here to serve fetid bodies, to bring healthy practices to those whose occupation has them taking their own health every night and selling it cheaply, maybe ten times; to those ugly, filthy ghosts whose flesh reeks of nauseating cheap perfume, who have saggy breasts, thighs with skin inflamed from scabies or ringworm or marked with scattered black circles, the historical vestiges of the syphilis germ.

We went straight inside.

This was the dormitory, a spacious room that had a wall in the middle that divided it into two sections. It had four rows of long platforms, placed contiguously, on top of which were rush mats and rattan headrests. Around them, from the floor up to the height of a person's head, the wall was painted black, which gave the room the gloomy look of a jail. The courtesans could store their belongings in the drawers at the head of the bed. Curious, I opened one and found a black woolen blanket, a container of face powder, and a comb. Two hundred places to sleep! The compartmentalized room was also divided in two with iron bars like a tiger cage! That was because years ago at night the women "with papers" would climb over the wall to beat the clandestine prostitutes because they were "trading without a license" and were illegally competing with them. It's true that there's no greater hatred than for those in the same profession. There were also a few women who had come from the provinces to work as servants but who fell into depravity, then got cuffed by the Girls' Squad. They had lain on these platforms, and each had known the power of a few of the women from the brothels who had struck and cursed them while yelling, "Your ancestors were whores! Do you know who we are? We have a license, we are government prostitutes!" So in went the iron bars.

The mayor was in a rush, so off we went.

This was the courtyard with an overhanging roof, where people could rest when it was very hot. There was a gramophone and "pickup" speaker for the women there, so that in their free time they could listen to such popular songs as "Anh Khoá" or "Văn Thiên Tường" in order to help lessen the sad burdens brought on by their misfortunes.

Crossing the courtyard, we came to a small room: the work room. Forty women making clothing all quickly stood up. They were barefoot with white pants, white short jackets; some had wool sweaters, others sleeveless sweaters, others no sweaters. It seemed as though they were completely expressionless. They did not look shy, nor did they look miserable because they had to stay in the Dispensary. This was the place where these women studied letters and their meanings, in addition to sewing. The government opened this room in 1935 in order to teach the women a trade so that afterward there would perhaps be a day when they hopefully could escape from prostitution. In many cases, because she had been forced to come and stay here, when a courtesan was released, she could read and write romanized Vietnamese script *(quốc ngữ)*. The women quietly went about their work.... The mayor finished his explanation. We entered another room.

The School of Sexual Prophylaxis! It's true: "getting it again" is the only significant problem with prostitutes. The classroom had desks, chairs, a blackboard, a raised platform, just like other classrooms.

Around the classroom were several rather luxurious bathrooms with sinks that the government, responding to the girls' desires to doll themselves up, used to teach them hygienic procedures. On the walls were inscribed several adages that encouraged people to keep their bodies clean, several large color drawings of the male and female sexual organs.... Several penises marked with pustules caused by syphilis, a few groins with horrible "mangoes."[6] Several vaginas, either undamaged or nauseatingly debased.... In these circumstances, the students are women who have worked in the brothels, and naturally the female teacher must be a nurse. When we walked in with the mayor, the instruction stopped because, from the teacher to the students, all folded their arms across their chests and stood up. Yet at other times, the classroom would resonate with the hygiene poem. Any woman who wants to win the prize and get out of the Dispensary must know it by heart....

Dr. Joyeux, at the time that he gave me the book *The Municipal Antivenereal Dispensary,* did not forget to give me the poem as a "gift."[7] And the mayor got one too. When the French had the idea of boasting about their efforts to eliminate venereal diseases, they asserted that "The Ballad of Eros" was a glorious achievement about which they were justified in being conceited. I therefore ask all of you men who are hypocritical or morally suspect to not smirk anymore, but let me do my job as a journalist.

Finally, the mayor took us into the inner courtyard. On the way we passed a row of bathing rooms with lotus blooms set up in Annamese style.

The inner courtyard was called the spacious garden. It had a pavilion that the Dispensary had finished putting up in the last few months. Previously you reached the end when you came to the bathing rooms, so the Dispensary women could not get fresh air and were locked in together under excessively cramped conditions. After several difficult negotiations with the general government, the city through much struggle arranged for the rent of three thousand square meters at the back of the Institute of Radium.[8] Now the Dispensary women have a large garden in which to practice planting vegetables and to entertain themselves with swings, hoops, balls, and exercises. There are times too when they play cards, although that is forbidden by the rules.

The visit was almost over, and the mayor wanted all of us to witness the solemn swearing of an oath to the Bạch My spirit by the madams and the girls who "have papers." Indeed, inside there is a little shrine dedicated to the spirit, and every day there are flowers and incense put upon it. An assistant physician called all of the madams in to swear that the authorities had given the women permission to leave for a few days to celebrate Tết but that they could not receive clients, make their still uncured diseases worse, or spread their diseases to the people.

Fifty girls stood in a long line before the shrine. The madams stood opposite them. People brought out mats. A madam rang a bell. Then one after another all of the madams and girls went to propitiate the spirit.

One madam, after she had propitiated the Bạch My spirit, came back and bowed before the mayor with her hands joined in front of her to show her thanks. Seeing me silently smile, Mr. Virgitti quickly explained, "Please do not think that the government is making them superstitious; it is that their superstitions have benefits for completing our work. If we let them out and do not force them to come back, we are afraid that they will act rashly, get greedy for money again, and then spread disease among the people."[9]

After that we took our leave.

It has to be acknowledged that thanks to the efforts of Mr. Virgitti and Dr. Joyeux, the women who are held in the Dispensary in the future will be treated in a much more humane manner than those in the past. But if these two men think that reforming the Dispensary's internal regime will make the five thousand clandestine prostitutes cease to panic when they hear the words lục xì, when there have already been more than enough orders for them to voluntarily come and submit to the Dispensary's rules, then both men are seriously mistaken!

The clandestine prostitutes have the playboys who are ready to pay them well. But what then are we to do to prevent these five thousand clandestine prostitutes from spreading disease among the masses?

Having arrived at this point, we must now chat with Mr. Mas, the inspector of the Girls' Squad.

6

The Girls' Squad

The guard at the Dispensary door, after looking suspiciously through a small round porthole, opened one side of the large doors for me.... It was 8:00 a.m. on Tuesday morning. It was not a morning for medical inspections, but in the office I saw Mr. Mas, the inspector of the Girls' Squad, and a crowd of ten girls.[1] Five officers were busy rummaging through papers. These women had papers but had fled without permission. Some had voluntarily returned to comply with the law; others had the law pick them up and bring them in. One man among the five Girls' Squad officers worked as a clerk.

One office with five officers and one inspector—that's all of the force that Hanoi can muster in the struggle against prostitution and venereal disease, so that's all there is to hunt down and arrest five thousand clandestine prostitutes or keep more than one hundred official prostitutes from doing ill-advised things on the streets. A truly deplorable state of affairs.... I couldn't help but think that although France had the Popular Front government and here we had Governor General Brévié, their lives were still like this.[2] The people doing this "government work" did not enjoy any of the labor law's benefits!

If the officers were kinder, it would be easy for me, because of their lamentable fate, to marshal a small part of my humble talents and write a piece entitled "The Glories and Humiliations of the Girls' Squad," in the spirit of Alfred de Vigny's *Servitude et Grandeur Militaires,* which now is Albert Sarraut's *Grandeur et Servitude Coloniales.*[3] But I know how suspicious these officers are of me! They haven't even seen me and they've already turned their backs! Journalist! Ah, tread carefully around a journalist because the press is an institution for hostile criticism, for slander, for exposing official corruption!

I had come into the room with a strong desire to meet the inspector.

Since he wasn't in, I couldn't ask him anything, so I had to furtively look at the officers and didn't dare say a word. The officers of the Girls' Squad looked like all the other Sûreté officers, a point symbolized in the pants they wore to ride their bicycles. People like this are obliged to perform some useful tasks, but as the continuing complaints showed, what nasty things had they done?

They had a number of duties: directly or indirectly implementing the laws restricting prostitution, stopping women from walking the streets, issuing or voiding the papers of the brothel women, checking out the red-numbered houses, maintaining the files and papers for the Police des Moeurs, and, on the "assigned days," keeping order and calling roll for all of the women with diseases in the Dispensary.... My word, those jobs; just calling them out makes a Vietnamese person's mouth tired. Yet there are only five people to shoulder this burden, so one must ask, when do they have the spare time to dream about a "forty-hour week"? And that's without mentioning harassing the people....

Indeed, if you want to do something bad to someone, you must have time to do it, no? Not to mention that for many years now, there have been only five people.

We are paying attention!

In the Police Law of May 18, 1915, Article 187 reads as follows:

A clandestine prostitution conviction results from an investigation of a woman by the Central Police Commissioner, in which all exculpatory evidence is carefully examined but she is nevertheless still shown to have engaged in one or more of the following acts:

1. Had frequent interactions with madams or registered prostitutes.
2. Was arrested by the Girls' Squad in an illegal house of prostitution on more than one occasion. 3. Was accused in a legal case of committing the offense of spreading venereal disease and having a doctor examine and confirm a venereal infection. 4. Invited, without reason, a number of men into the home when the woman was unmarried; married but the husband was absent; or lacked a steady means of livelihood.[4]

Do you see it yet? The law on a piece of paper is one thing; its implementation is something else. With Article 187 of the Police Law the members of the Girls' Squad acquired many powers.

That already was the case, but with the decision of February 3, 1921, Resident Superior Rivet signed another law that was even scarier because it was even more vague and indeterminate:

Article 34: Prostitution is an occupation that involves supplying the body to any man with the purpose of obtaining money; the offense of practicing prostitution without a license can be confirmed after examining all of the evidence, and the task of producing all exculpatory evidence has been relegated to the offending individual.[5]

That's dangerous! That's dangerous!

With two legal articles like this and an uneducated people that anyone can bully, the officers of the "Girls' Squad" can do whatever they want! In the implementation of the law, the abuse of authority for dishonest advantage or the proper execution of one's responsibilities becomes an issue of individual conscience.

◆◆◆

Given this situation, several years ago during a 1930 session of the Municipal Council, the responsible authorities discussed measures to eliminate prostitution before a group of doctors that included Dr. Joyeux, Dr. Piquemal, the assistant physician Trần Văn Lai, the pharmacist Lafon, Dr. De Raymond, Dr. Gaide, etc.... The mayor had received from Dr. Le Roy des Barres a letter of apology for not attending the meeting in which he wrote the following:

> I consider that up to now in 1930, the policy that we have been using has not had any greater results than in earlier years. Moreover, if the budget does not allot a large amount of money, then the method of eradication by legal means will be completely ineffective. Aside from that, in a locality in which the people have the character they have here—in that when there is bribery, it is bribery without end—the people resent it, and we must recognize that things can happen as a result.
>
> Because of those latter traits, fifteen years ago people brought into the Dispensary a girl of about thirteen or fourteen who had been falsely accused of working as a clandestine prostitute. After the investigation had started, it came out that an Annamese detective of the Girls' Squad, after being unable to rape the young girl, thought that there was nothing better than arresting her and sending her to the Dispensary to avoid having legal action brought against him.
>
> In my opinion, even if we establish further laws, we will not be able to implement them because it will create a false peace that will become the source of countless other illegalities and harassment.

That is an "opinion" about the "Girls' Squad" that we have stated already. But are there other men among the "high officials" who have no sympathy for that unit? Here are the words of Dr. Le Dantec:

> Here we have only one Frenchman working for the Police des Moeurs. Instead of that number, there must be more for it to function adequately. Approximately how many are necessary for all of Indochina? To give an example, what if the government recruits more people? Over and above everything else, there would be one matter that would be difficult to resolve: if there is recruitment, then it can involve only Frenchmen because we more than understand the mind of the Annamites, and as such we cannot allow them to be involved in this work, for reasons that are not really necessary to state (*BSMCI,* April 1912).

Then came the turn of Dr. Gauducheau, who was even fiercer:

> When an unfortunate young girl must sell her body to feed herself, then the government immediately pounces on her and forces her to pay taxes, and there are people who say that is inhumane. After near starvation comes humiliation.... And then comes the turn of the native detective to torment her in the course of executing his duties; not only does he watch out for illegal activities, but he also looks out for the amount of money he can acquire in the brothel! People want to talk about the reform of the Girls' Squad. That is impossible. People cannot reform a disaster for the people. The only option is for them to get rid of it. (*BSMCI,* February 1915)

Up until 1925, this unit of the police had been bitterly criticized. Dr. Coppin, a director of the Dispensary who held the post before Dr. Joyeux, wrote the following:

> As for prostitution, we should not hide from the people the cancer that is the Police des Moeurs. In the past and today, any country that has the legal regulation of prostitution still has people that protest, and in this country it is even more disastrous. Especially when people understand the mentality of the Annamites who work for the government, for whom everything is about money. No matter how carefully they are investigated, the members of the Girls' Squad still take bribes to put off the search for clandestine prostitutes, and because of that, when we see who is arrested, it is those who do not have a penny in their pockets! (*BSMCI,* June 1925)[6]

There they are, the words of a man who bitterly criticized the Girls' Squad here. But whose words are they? Surely they come from the Annamese masses? No! They are the words of the Frenchmen that we commoners refer to as the "mandarins." That's right; it's not a member of the Girls' Squad. When we hear those men speak of the Annamese mentality and mind, who among us isn't completely ashamed? So in the civilized countries—take France, for example—is this service evaluated positively or negatively?

On this point, a passage from the newspaper *L'Oeuvre,* run by Monsieur Daladier, who is currently the minister of defense of our "mother country."[7]

The men of the Service des Moeurs search out and throw into jail only those poor women who still walk the streets at night or go into bars or the shabby hotels. These women have no families, have no one to protect them, and mistakenly think that through prostitution we can help them to escape from hunger and privation.

In Paris, there are currently sixty thousand women who every day survive on prostitution. Yet there are not even six thousand young women whose names are in the police register. That service arrests only those who are not clever, who do not have the money to escape from humiliation, meaning those who are simple, thick, "defective." ... Forcing them to carry papers is imprudent and also unfair because it is only the poor who bear that humiliating stigma. That obligation has a further danger because it forces a woman who unwillingly works as a prostitute for a short period to work as one her whole life. It only serves to increase the size of the prostitute army, an army from which they can never desert nor escape. (*L'Oeuvre,* September 5, 1933)

Dear readers, we have been given permission to shrug our shoulders and take a deep breath. On this point, East and West have met up.

◆◆◆

I am very sad because I don't get to see the inspector at all.

Madam Limongi, the chief supervisor for the Dispensary, could see what I was uneasy about.[8] So, with Dr. Đặng Hanh Kiên, she showed me a statute that had recently been amended.

Was it happy news or sad news?

In the past, a member of the Girls' Squad, relying upon Article 187 of the decree of May 18, 1915, could force anyone to go into the Dispensary, according to his individual discretion. Now it seems that the members of the

Girls' Squad lack the authority to do their job because if they want to arrest a *demi-mondaine* and take her to the Dispensary, they have to take turns and find a way to catch her directly in the act of selling herself a minimum of four times. If a *demi-mondaine* has been caught eight times, but not in the act, she still does not need to fear getting "papers."

Because of that, there are some five thousand prostitutes in Hanoi today, but the number who "have papers" is only one hundred and nineteen.

If I were to ask Dr. Joyeux, he would respond:

> The members of the Girls' Squad cannot carry out their work very well for two reasons. The first is that the contemporary legal statutes are unclear, and we have already passed the point at which being able to enact a law is the same as being able to implement it. The second is that the service has already been so heavily discredited that it has reached a point in which the men in charge do not dare to believe the men under their authority any longer.

As it turns out, due to a fear of abuses of authority by the detectives, the director of the Sûreté keeps an eye on this service, and even though he knows that people sometimes level slanderous accusations against it, he needs to remain circumspect and amend the misdemeanor infractions in Article 187 of the law mentioned above.

Only after four times are they forced to go to the Dispensary! And only after eight times... do they have to work in a brothel.

Now where are the women who have no money but yearn to wear the Lemur tunic?[9] And where are the romantic women who Mayor Virgitti complained endorsed "prostitution for prostitution's sake"? They certainly do not stand in the "art for humanity's sake" faction do they?

I had already thought to myself, "Perhaps it is better if the officers of the Girls' Squad abuse their authority...."

I reminded Madam Limongi of the saying, "Fear of the *gendarmes* is the beginning of wisdom." She shrugged her shoulders and smiled.

The scourge of prostitution, a malignant tumor that is difficult to treat, stuck in a vicious circle....

Now the officers of the Girls' Squad are no longer the terror of corrupted and debauched girls.

Sisters, long live love!

7

Women of the Book of Sorrows

Victor Hugo said, "In humanity, there is no one who is so pure that they have never been punished." Anatole France wrote, "Naiveté is usually only more luck than righteousness." The philosopher Esquirol took that sentence even further: "People who are even in a small measure rich in feeling can perhaps fully recognize that in spite of having a very clear conscience, a person can still be imprisoned or exiled, and because of that, people must pay attention to the fate of the imprisoned."[1]

Those were some of the ideas that unexpectedly came to mind when I, for the third time, entered the Dispensary with the desire to realistically describe the lives of the brothel women held within. It's true that in comparison to upstanding women, these women can perhaps be called women who have been sentenced, who deserve their punishments, if there are punishments that merit harsh treatment, if there is harsh treatment....

Thus, if a young girl wants to be put into the Dispensary, all she has to do is trifle with passion through thoughts of liberation, free marriage, Europeanization, etc.... There will undoubtedly be a revolution in the family if she has an "unworthy" husband or excessive credulousness toward her lover—"I will commit suicide if I cannot marry him"—and then she is deceived and then is excessively reckless.... Or she does not know her place and only has a little bit of money in her pocket, but she longs for lots of jewelry on her hands, around her neck. She starts to believe in novels and becomes a bit "romantic," and then love takes precedence over all in her life, and her life is ruined. To summarize in one sentence, it takes only a little bit, and then an upstanding young girl will have her name written in the Book of Sorrows.[2]

I want to say it like Esquirol did: "Honest women should pay attention to the impure women."

Dear Sirs, look and see! Over there, a group of women, most of whom are nicely plump, yet their complexions are pale and sallow, the coarse garments of the Dispensary make them look disgusting, and the body of each is full of either the gono, the spiro, or the Ducrey germ.[3] But here's what's hard to understand. They are still plump as if they were normal! Those debauched women, chatting in the courtyard, sitting and studying "The Ballad of Eros" in the School of Sexual Prophylaxis, lining up together to wait for their injection of 914 in the assistant physician's treatment room, swinging in the spacious courtyard—all have faces without a trace of worry, full of life, without a care, to the point that if you were like me at that moment, you would be uneasy and uncertain about the chaotic reactions in your mind.[4] Are they feelings of compassion or disdain? This woman has a face that looks simple, rustic, dim-witted. That woman has a sly air; she definitely "knows what life is." That one has a swagger, a rough one at that; she might hit a black French soldier on Hàng Mành Street…take a look! A disordered and unruly slice of humanity, worthy of both disgust and compassion. An element of society in which the god of lust, or hunger and deprivation, has shattered the existing social order and rearranged it as one group. A stratum of people who have sacrificed their lives for good morality and customs so that society will less frequently experience incidents of adultery, rape, and depravity; and they have heroically sacrificed, but nobody knows! A few women who have been lost in an experiment, enduring misfortune so that society can by turns be renovated, and yet it makes us frown and feel sick at heart to think that some men think that there are only two good things in life, liquor and women!

This is their novel?

The plight of each girl is perhaps the same. The girls who came from the countryside, or who forsook their husbands because they had to taste the bait of modern living, or who left the provinces to work as servants but did not succeed, or whose hearts started pounding when, as they were sitting on the sidewalk, hungry and thirsty, a few Hanoi "dandies" with caring attitudes tenderly spoke false words into their ears. A cad next to a "lost cow" who is straight from the countryside and 100 percent "certain."[5] As for the girl born and bred in the city…she finds a lover—"The willow character is misshapen, though the love appointed by heaven has yet to appear"—is disowned by mother and father, deceived by her lover, an "unlucky fate" like that.[6] Despite being from the city, or the country, or being corrupted, or being hungry and thirsty, all of these girls became victims of the cunning schemes of the old hags who run the opium dens, the boys in the seedy hotels, the pimps, or the nighttime rickshaw drivers, all of whom spin a frightful spider's web to get them to work at the nearly four hundred *rooms for rent* scattered throughout Hanoi!

I wanted to call over a few girls to ask some questions. The chief supervisor of the Dispensary, speaking in French, quickly stopped me. "They won't answer at all. Your newspaper at one point referred to them as 'prostitutes' *(gái đĩ)*, so they were very unhappy. Why didn't you choose a gentler word? Even in here, no one on the staff refers to them as prostitutes."

Ah! So I have stumbled onto humanity's terrible pride! It was my mistake, my enormous mistake! *How can you call a prostitute a prostitute?* Instead I must call them, for example…the Muse, or…anything else is better.

I immediately smiled and asked the chief supervisor, "Madam, so I do not have the right to call something by its name?"

"You could perhaps call them, for example, *'demi-mondaines' (gái giang hồ)."*

I had to laugh because if they have been stuck in here, how can they be in the *"demi-monde!"* So sometimes when you read, you will notice that I have to use the word "brothel" *(thanh lâu),* even though they wear the Lemur-style tunic, even though we are far from the time when Nguyễn Du wrote, "Seven tricks to catch a man, eight tricks to please a man.…Juice from a pomegranate rind and the blood of a cockscomb.…She'd change the flowers and lay on her mat."[7] He did not know of the modern Kiềus, whose lives involve Gonacrine, 914, Dmelcos, the Dispensary's duck's bill (speculum), the laws that restrict prostitution, or the Girls' Squad.

I wanted to see if the chief supervisor's advice was true or not, so I had already slightly opened the bamboo blinds on the office window. The girls who were sitting and chatting in the entryway to the pavilion, and those who waited for medication in the room of Assistant Physician Đặng Hanh Kiên, all scowled and glanced angrily at me. It was true. I was under suspicion, detested. I could ask nothing further. I immediately asked Madam Limongi, "Madam, in the time that you have been in charge of the Dispensary, what has been your impression of those women over there, of prostitution? Please be kind enough to answer, especially on the issue that you do not want me to call them prostitutes, even though they officially are prostitutes. I want to see if their indignation is legitimate."

The chief supervisor went about her work of sorting out note cards that recorded the names of women in the Dispensary and had drawings of vaginas with blue and red pencil markings on them (markings that recorded the condition of each patient's disease). She did not respond immediately. Suddenly the government's "Ballad of Eros" resounded from the classroom as several dozen of Nurse Nghĩa's students happily recited it together, spurring me to remember the times when I was a student…in a group recitation hour.

If you are suspicious, then don't do it;
That danger will enter your body;
Think ahead, don't be greedy for what is now;
If you find anyone who is a thousand times certain, then it's okay.
Though the client doesn't have the slightest sign of disease,
Clean as a glass, but wants to go for a long time,
Don't listen, for the harm comes later.
Who is happy? He that just brought us sorrow!

They stopped a moment, then stridently continued.

Maybe the client has already paid his money,
But only have sex the proper way!
As soon as it is over,
Soap and iodine on the places it flowed.

I could not deny the utility of a song like this. Among the brothel women, there were many who, perhaps because they were lazy, or perhaps because they were dim-witted, have never known anything of hygienic methods. Such ignorance allows venereal diseases to run wild among 90 percent of the common people, a lustful people deserving of shame, a people who have reached the point that they should be called the people of Sodom and Gomorrah. The proof for that can be seen in the venereal disease advertisements that fill all of the newspapers. But I have the right to be surprised when I see women of that type, who have to learn a song like that, get indignant when they hear me call them by their name! After explaining apologetically, I spoke again with the chief supervisor.

"Madam, I am aware of the opinions of such renowned individuals as Le Roy des Barres, Coppin, Joyeux, Virgitti, on the renovation, the ignorantly conducted Westernization, of my society. These men have all held the desire for material things in great contempt as it has given rise to immoral practices among our people. Prostitution is for the most part the bitter fruit of that depravity. Now, if I could know more of your opinions, the opinions of a woman who must treat that wound, my investigation would be finished completely!"

Madam Limongi quickly shrugged her shoulders and said, "I do not want to pass judgment upon the Annamese as those officials who are senior to me have. It's very hard to say."

"Madam, those debauched women over there, what are the things that led them to this place? Destitution or moral corruption?"

The chief supervisor immediately responded. "I believe that for most of them it is destitution. I know them very well, and most of them are country girls, unemployed. Maybe there are some who are corrupted, but not 'corrupted' according to the Western meaning of the word!"

At that moment a woman in very elegant clothing, a pair of Charles IX high-heeled shoes, a very fashionable chestnut-colored overcoat, and the gait of a noblewoman gracefully walked across the courtyard to leave the Dispensary. Surprised, I looked over to ask about her. The chief supervisor explained: "That is a woman from outside who comes here to learn how to make clothing with the women who have diseases and are being held here. They have free time so they voluntarily come in to learn, and freely come in and out, because the government set up a section for learning a trade so that perhaps in the future they can escape from prostitution. Of course, we must allow any woman in who wants to come here to learn."

When she finished speaking, she had to go to another room because of her work. As I wanted to know what a day was like for a Dispensary girl, I rummaged around for the decree that Mayor Douguet signed August 9, 1928.[8]

Every morning the women must get up at 6:00 a.m. They wash their faces or bathe and wash their hair. Then they go to the examination room for an injection. The tasks they must perform include sweeping out their lodgings, washing their clothes, doing their sewing, etc. Their meals include rice, beef, pork, vegetables, and tofu, which are brought in by an employee of the Hôpital Indigène. They are forbidden to drink alcohol, smoke opium, argue, shout, or gamble. If they want to smoke cigarettes or chew betel nut, they have to receive permission from the chief supervisor. If they break the rules, they are fined, or their food is withheld, or they are held in solitary confinement for a maximum of eight days. If they flee, they are also punished with confinement. If they come back voluntarily, they are held for four days; if they are captured and brought back, eight days.

This decree had been changed and had had many clauses added, particularly after Mayor Virgitti's reforms.

That is a perfunctory description of everyday life inside the Dispensary, wherein the women whose names are inscribed in the Book of Sorrows, as well as those who still do not "have papers," must be confined until their diseases are cured and where they must eat and live all thrown together. Two hundred women in a private world! A communal life in which every hour and every minute is controlled down to the smallest detail. Two hundred miserable people, with no loved ones, whose mistake was to become ensnared by passion, or who did not want to starve to death. They come in here to fix their tools to make them healthy again, so that when they go out they can again serve the urges of the carpenter, the rickshaw driver, the awkward Vietnamese soldier, the black-skinned drunk. Two hundred people confined when five thousand other people, of the same occupation, can freely spread every venereal disease! Two hundred people who are confined because they worked as prostitutes, while at the same time numerous other prostitutes are still known as miss, madam, esteemed lady!

It is a truly unfair aspect of society, and I say *of society,* not of the Hanoi mayor's office. Because of this, in a debate over policies to deal with prostitution, Georges Clemenceau, the hero of the French people who saved France, had to raise his voice and argue with Senator Bérenger as follows:[9]

What is a proper marriage if not a structure for the buying and selling of sex allowed by law? When an average daughter receives millions in dowry, we can see that she has been turned into a commodity, even in spite of herself. She knows or does not know the covetous desires she arouses in the customers, who are the marquises, the counts, the dukes, or the parliamentarians who might become ministers or have already been ministers. They touch her, turn her around, to evaluate her. I want people to explain to me so I can understand: why is this buying and selling, which is respectable, more honorable than the selling of sex?

Do people dare to state with certainty that this system is less worthy of shame than the other because it has been beautified, praised, and encouraged? But from a blind millionairess to a middle-class girl whose family is endlessly adding to her dowry as they seek someone to betroth her to, alas, do you know how debased love is when tainted by the smell of money! What method, therefore, should be used to deal with this situation, dear Senator of the strictest morals who vaguely worries over a type of society that is not like what you have imagined, Sir? It is certainly not the method of regulating prostitution because you are a person who dares bother only the women who work as prostitutes because they are poor and hungry, yet you leave alone the prostitutes with diamonds who work as prostitutes every day, every month, every year, all of their lives!

Thus, is it true that there are girls and women who dare to be arrogant enough to say they do not ... engage in prostitution?[10]

Just as Clemenceau's idea stated, it is only the women who have a profession, or who have jobs, who can avoid the label of "working as prostitutes." A bitter truth that will offend many women! No, it's not only the Dispensary girls who work as prostitutes.

Yet it is the two hundred Dispensary girls over there who have to carry on their shoulders the bad name of the whole group.... The girls of the Book of Sorrows!

No, the Dispensary is not a place full of ordeals for the prostitutes. The place full of ordeals is outside, in the damp and foul-smelling houses on Hàng Thịt Street, Hàng Mành Street, Đào Duy Từ Street, Án Sát Siêu Alley, of the land of a thousand-year civilization. Love for money.... If you want to know the physical indignities caused by the love that is tainted by the smell of money, of the Dispensary girls after they have sold their flesh, then we must wait until the day of the medical examinations.

8

Medical Examination Day

Throughout the morning on Wednesdays and Fridays, the Dispensary guards do not bolt the door shut but merely close it.[1] These are the "scheduled" days. From 7:00 a.m. until 8:30 a.m., about fifty rickshaws stop in front of the gray door of a building that holds within an untold number of secrets. The rickshaws come from all directions and gather there: Hàng Thịt Alley, Yên Thái Alley, Gia Ngư Street, Đào Duy Từ Street, Cửa Đông Street, Đường Thành, Nam Ngư Alley, Án Sát Siêu Alley.... From these rickshaws descend some eighty women. (That is one-half of the people from Hanoi's "brothel world"; the other half comes on the other scheduled day as each week has two scheduled days.)

If you have business at the court or on Julien Blanc Street, go straight past in a serious manner; don't gawk or stare. "Do not stare at illicit goods," as a learned scholar once stated. Our brothel women are still self-conscious, despite the fact that their occupation obliges them to sacrifice that self-consciousness some ten times every night. Don't tease the disciples of Bạch My, or he will... be embarrassed about them.

They come to meet the "duck's bill," the symbol of the Dispensary—and of prostitution. If you want to see the physical indignities of the prostitution trade, you must see a medical examination session.

"What the hell are they going to do?"

There are some girls with withered faces and new clothes. There are some with clean faces and worn, dirty clothes. Some wind their hair plainly, with a Huế-style gold necklace. Others let their hair hang free, curled and dyed red. Still others wear very fashionable overcoats. Some lips are painted in the shape of a heart. Some eyebrows run in a slanted line like those of Mai Lan Phương.[2] Some eyelids are ringed in black like Greta Garbo's, all on the fat or thin faces of girls from Đình Bảng, Cầu Lim, Phùng, Noi, etc.[3] ... Yet the moon and wind of Hanoi, the city of a thousand-year civilization, cannot fully transform them. Still, by chance, there might be a few among those eighty girls who have the simple-heartedness and fascinating charm of Tuyết in Khái Hưng's book *Đời Mưa Gió*.[4] The gray door opens then closes again, closes then opens again, to let them swiftly rush in. There is not a single time when people crossing the street can clearly see the guard's face.

There! A glittering private car has just stopped. A fair-complected man, short and fat like a Japanese, has just stepped out of the car. He wears a gray-ish-blue suit, with brightly shining black shoes. The door opens, the guard stands straight and deferentially prepares to greet the man. It is the doctor.

I quicken my pace and lift my hat.

Mr. Nguyễn Huy Quỳnh quickly turns around.

"Ah! Hello Mr. . . . *Tương Lai*."[5]

Assistant Physician Nguyễn Huy Quỳnh could be regarded a learned scholar, if we defined the term by all of his "knowledge" about society's infamies. With the outward appearance of an upstanding bourgeois gentleman, here was a man who through his profession clearly understood the depraved situation of our Hanoi people, more than a revolutionary party member, more than a man gone broke through dissolute living.

One day, because he wanted to put an end to the pestering of a journalist who frequently snuck around and bothered him by asking to meet with him, the director of the Municipal Hygiene Service, Dr. Joyeux, cast me off to his capable subordinate, Assistant Physician Nguyễn Huy Quỳnh. I secretly rejoiced because here was a person who could potentially explain everything I needed to know. But Mr. Quỳnh was never free. How many times had I gone to see him at the mayor's office, but he was out traveling all over the city to deal with an encephalitis problem or certify a death or certify a birth or inspect various sites in the city. As such, getting him to meet with me was very difficult.

Today, therefore, I was able to "capture" Mr. Quỳnh as he was about to go into battle against all of the catastrophes caused by the Bạch My spirit!

Dear reader, we are stepping into the Dispensary with the doctor. Let's go!

◆◆◆

Everything had been prepared and "put in its place" in the examination room. It was exactly 9:00 a.m. A zinc-covered table, a chair on each side to let the women climb up and down. Two nurses had lit an alcohol stove that held twenty "duck's bills" whose cotton wrapping had already been removed. On this side of the examination table were Chief Supervisor Limongi and Assistant Physician Đặng Hanh Kiên. They asked for the "Book of Sorrows" for all the girls. On the other side was an officer of the Girls' Squad, sitting at another small table with the cards that recorded the disease conditions. Inspector Mas and four other members of his unit kept going in and out in order to keep very strict order.

The doctor, Mr. Quỳnh, had taken off his suit coat and was wearing a white smock. Upon his head was a white cloth cap, somewhat like the kind worn by chefs in the big hotels. He sat down and thrust his hands into a pair of rubber gloves that stretched to his elbows! Inspector Mas then began by calling the name of one madam, who was then to call out the names of all the girls in her house.

Outside of the examination room, under the pavilion's overhang, the girls had stripped off all of their outer clothing, untied their shoes, and taken off their pants. The only thing they had left on was a brassiere or a short, lightweight shirt. It was a truly strange sight. Seventy or eighty "blooms who know how to speak," with hair wound with velvet, or parted on the side Huế-style, or up in a bun Saigon-style. Their faces properly powdered, their lip-stick properly applied, with gold or heart-shaped necklaces about their necks, hands with rings of green or red jade, and brassieres or short tunics upon their midsections, but...for the bottom half, they were all nudists! The officers of the Girls' Squad released long, dispirited yawns—what a pity!—as they went back and forth among this group of tiny women. They kept an eye out so that the girls did not mix up their clothing or find a way to conceal their diseases through methods that the Dispensary's private dictionary describes as *maquillage*.[6]

Concealing a disease? Would women such as these, who have complied with all of the laws of prostitution, of the Dispensary, who on their scheduled date have come here, still want to find a way to conceal a disease? Can it be like that?

Yes, perhaps. Because if the examination reveals that a woman has a dis-ease, she will be held in the Dispensary, to her loss. She will have no "work to do," which means she won't have a penny to spend. The prize money from the voluptuaries is but a few dozen cents, but the poverty of the red-num-bered houses is indescribable: the women of the brothels, outside of two daily meals, don't get a penny of the owner's general profits. And yet, they still need to get pants, shirts, fake necklaces, velvet to tie up their hair.... Moreover, when a woman has a lover she passionately loves, a launderer or barber, for example, when *she* has to stay in the Dispensary, and *he* is on the outside, she suffers more than Kim Trọng.[7] It's true: they still crave love, those who sell their love cheaply ten times a day. And there's one more thing about the madams. Say a madam has ten girls under her to receive clients every day, but in going to the Dispensary she loses four or five girls. If she knows on a Sunday night, when the exam is a few days away, that a girl has caught something, she will send her out to deal with the ten menacing French soldiers who are tall and black like the pillars of a burned house—and who may be brutal as well if they are drunk.

◆◆◆

So the officers of the Girls' Squad must keep an eye on the girls to prevent them from concealing their diseases.

Here is Dr. Coppin's description of the methods of disguise:

On the medical examination days, from early morning, as soon as the girls wake up, they wash their vaginas with lukewarm water that has alum mixed in. After the washing, one girl among them takes both of her fists and presses on the abdomen of the diseased girl to evacuate the contents of her uterus (?) [*sic*]; then she will take a corner of a handkerchief or rolled paper and place it into the cervix or the urethra, and it is held there until the time comes when she needs to get onto the examination table.

To conclude the preparations and for greater security, smokers or not, the girls will smoke one or two pipes of opium before presenting themselves at examination (more than one-third of the women with papers are opium smokers).

Certain girls prefer infusions of betel leaf boiled in water, which they find more efficacious. With these two methods, the mucosa of the uterus becomes whiter, the redness of the cervix diminishes significantly, and the uterine secretions decrease.

Finally, if in spite of these methods the secretions still turn the handkerchief-tampon yellow, very sick women have recourse to a final method; it consists of inserting into the vagina noncoagulated pig's blood, which can be ordered from a butcher, in order to simulate menstruation.

For chancres and ulcerations, they employ three procedures, depending upon their severity. For the least serious lesions, they are content to wash the damaged mucosa with a solution that has a very high concentration of alum. For more severe lesions, the method is more complicated: after the initial washing with an alum solution, they apply the following powder to the wound: calcinated alum that is ground into fine powder and mixed, in unknown proportions, with a powder that comes from *sapèques* (an alloy of tin and zinc).[8] This powder, which is both absorbent and astringent, renders the mucosa its natural color. Finally, the last method is the most widely practiced and costs nothing; one crushes between one's fingers the flowers of the red hibiscus and applies the juice on the infected region, which has previously been cleaned. This procedure is currently very popular because the hibiscus blooms year round.[9]

Those are the methods that the government—through the meticulous investigations of M. Trinh Huu Loi, a capable assistant of Mr. Coppin—discovered among the disciples of Bạch My in 1925.

Do the women still use those methods in 1937? Who knows! The government is always conservative and follows old customs. And the officers of the Girls' Squad must still be as thorough as usual.

One girl has a handkerchief in her hand, another has a meaningless scrap of paper. An officer of the Girls' Squad angrily glares at them. "Put away that handkerchief! Get rid of that paper now!"

They empty their hands, two white palms, and go up to the "duck's bill." No, don't make something of this! Don't say anything! Don't snicker!

Inside, Inspector Mas, with the heavy accent of a Frenchman, calls roll. "Trane Ti Lock!"

"Yes!"

"N'guyen Ti Yane! N'guyen Ti Suan! Phame Ti Ti!"

Trần Thị Lộc, Nguyễn Thị Yên, Nguyễn Thị Sửu, Phạm Thị Tý....

So it basically went. As I heard them, those names sounded so innocent, names that many times in the distant past had been fondly uttered from the mouth of a gentle mother; in worry from the mouth of a father, like a rooster caring for his offspring; or in plaintive anguish from the mouth of a young lover. Now those names came from the mouth of an inspector of the Girls' Squad, wrapped in the thick accent of a Frenchman trying to speak our language.

The doctor, who wore on his head a steel ring of the same type as the speculum, turned to the duck's bill. Thị Lộc climbed up, laid down on the table on her back, and pulled up her brassiere. The nurse pressed an electrical button;... from one part of the "duck's bill" a silvery light illuminated the darkness. Science has brought light into the inner royal chambers, the hidden place that holds the Bạch My spirit's precious belongings. Not to worry! Thị Lộc is disease-free. The duck's bill is removed and tossed into a pot for boiling; then the director examines other parts of her body. Thị Lộc, an intelligent courtesan with personality, is not concealing a disease, so this examination is routine. She steps down from the table and heads out to the overhang in the pavilion with a thrilled expression.

The nurse gets another "duck's bill."

Madam Limongi puts a clean hygiene history card before the doctor. Assistant Physician Kiên stamps it with a seal after scribbling a few words on it. He then hands it to the madam, a rich person, but also not in the least bit rich.

Now it is Thị Yên's turn.

Seeing that her lips are stained red from betel, the director looks over at the madam. Thị Yên is chewing betel! Go rinse your mouth out completely, and do it fast! Chewing betel, that's a way to conceal a disease, so in a moment the doctor will be required to conduct an extremely careful examination. The syphilis germ sometimes eats into the teeth, gums, cheeks, lips. The doctor is now obliged to examine not only below, but above too.

Thị Sửu looks suspicious. After the "duck's bill" comes a bamboo stick with cotton wrapped around one end that is used to check further. They see the place where the cotton smears something wet and somewhat golden-colored. They then smear the wet part on a small piece of glass and then mark the piece of glass with a secret number. For the sake of convenience, as they are already suspicious, they take a blood sample from Thị Sửu, and the vial of her blood will also have a secret number. Secret? Here Dr. Joyeux explained to me, "I had to think up a way to make secret markings because of the disgraceful atmosphere of bribery that surrounds me. It reached such an extent that confinement was being hindered as the examinations were not having their intended consequences." Those vials of blood or pieces of glass will go to the Pasteur Institute or to the microscope in the Hygiene Room at the mayor's office. If those containers holding the blood clearly recorded the person's name, a madam could grease the palm of the nurse to get her to make a false declaration to her superiors so her girl would escape confinement.

Thị Sửu looked doubtful; then the doctor gave the order: "*Isolement* (Isolation)!"

That word meant that the person would be temporarily confined, without permission to await adjudication on the outside. In here, the doctor is also an official of the court. People can be held after being denounced by only a little piece of cotton stained with some dirty fluid.

Now it is Thị Tý's turn.

Right after the vagina comes the anus. Removing the cotton produces enough material to clearly indict her. Angrily the doctor glares at the madam and rails at her: "She already has a disease! How can you allow that? Don't you remember what the officials recommended, or what?"

The madam, Thị Tý's boss, the person responsible, clasps her hands together and objects. "Sir, I didn't know anything at all! I can't do anything!"

Madam Limongi hands Thị Tý's card to Dr. Quỳnh. He makes a wry face and scolds her; "In 1933, she was already sick one time. The government had to treat her for three months before she was released. How can you let her receive clients like this?"

Thị Tý had at that point already stepped down from the table. She was crying as she responded.

"Sir, it's not like that; he would have strangled and killed me!"

"Then you should have called the police!"

"Sir…but, he'd already taken my clothes off!"

"So you didn't call anyone for help, eh?"

"Sir, it was in a seedy hotel, not at my brothel. That day the hotel had no guests."

The madam butts in, "Sir, at my brothel I would have called the police immediately!"

"So he was a…?"

"Sir, he was a black man."

Thị Tý is escorted out. The doctor gives the madam a container of Pommade de Duret.

To treat the disease? No, to smear on the anus to prevent disease! My goodness! The useful wares of the god of lust even involve the anus! Dr. Joyeux, in his investigations, had already had to raise his voice in a long lament:

> When I say that they (the soldiers) have that disease, it is because most of them go to the anus, and I am not exaggerating because in 1930, I found that 41 percent had infected anuses, and in 1931 and 1932, approximately 30 percent of the patients had to be confined because they had chancres or boils in their colons. Only Western soldiers prefer to have sex this way, a way that the women detest, but they are forced to submit to it. The point worth noting is that even though the officers castigate them, the soldiers argue that due to their fear of contracting a venereal disease, they must reluctantly practice sodomy.[10]

The germ of the sodomy scourge is the Ducrey bacillus, which, along with the gonorrhea germ, devastates the anus as it does the reproductive organs.[11] There are cases in which some brothel girls can simultaneously have all three venereal germs, gono, spiro, and Ducrey, in the vagina, anus, and mouth!

9

Student and Teacher

On December 2, 1933, the governor general signed a decision establishing for Indochina a Committee for the Elimination of Venereal Diseases. On May 2, 1934, at the request of Mayor Virgitti, the government set up an organization called the Prophylactic League (Ligue Prophylactique), whose goal it was to investigate this complex problem in the Hanoi region, implement the hundreds of opinions that people had put forth for dealing with prostitution, and then convey to the committee the results of the methods that had been experimented with in order to determine if they could be applied to all of Indochina. The league was recognized by governmental decision on October 26, 1934. The president was of course the mayor of Hanoi. The board of directors was composed of representatives from the various institutions that had contributed money. The minister of colonies, in an acknowledgment of the league's utility, added an annual subsidy of ten thousand francs.[1] Apart from its other tasks, the league reformed the Dispensary. And thanks to the committee's efforts, inside the Dispensary there was a strange school called the School of Sexual Prophylaxis (École de Prophylaxie Sexuelle).[2]

Dear readers, please do not think that this school is like hundreds of thousands of others. We know it has tables, a raised platform, a blackboard, and chairs to sit in, but the standard placards featuring geography and the natural sciences have been replaced with drawings of naked male and female bodies, healthy or diseased, along with diagrams of male and female sexual organs, drawn in their natural colors and in the detail desired by anatomists. Around the classroom there are eight washrooms. Every room has nineteen drawers to hold the items the students use (washcloth, soap, all kinds of medications, and all of the items used in douching); a large mirror; a Western-style wash basin—everything is of the most luxurious quality. Behind the blackboard in a private room are barrels that hold water for bathing. Studying isn't all that students do in this strange school. They put what they learn into practice as well.

But what do they study?

They study… to be prostitutes. If you want to become a good prostitute, the most important thing to understand is hygiene because if you are unclean, you will disastrously spread venereal diseases to your race. But if you want to become a good prostitute, alas, it requires so much work! The program of study is as follows:

Part One

Introduction to the Status of Women in Society and the Prostitution Trade. Methods for washing the face, hair, and hands. Bathing. Methods for washing the sexual organs. Douching.

Part Two

Anatomical Description of the Male and Female Sexual Organs. Pregnancy and childbirth. Venereal diseases, infectious diseases, and their dreadful consequences. Venereal disease symptoms on men. On women. Useful methods for treating diseases.[3]

Outside of these scientific matters, there is also a statement on the goals of hygiene, and with "The Ballad of Eros," the Muse brings these "melodious and magical" verses to lead science by the hand to battle against the Bạch My spirit's awful consequences. The government has sought out every way to fight the ignorance that torments the prostitutes only because they are shy. Doctor Joyeux has stated the following:

> It is true that one surprising fact that we recognize about Annamese women, including even the common prostitute, is that they all have a deep and unreasonable shyness. Because of that, when a woman with papers, due to her occupation, offers up her body (and it is never happily offered up) to all of the mischievousness of a lustful client, she is still not comfortable exposing her sexual organs. As a result, an Annamese prostitute never has the shameless provocative attitude of a Western prostitute. For example, an Annamite woman will never, regardless of class, sleep naked; at a minimum she must keep her baggy pants on. This fact explains why they are so scared of the medical examination.

This traditional sense of shame, if it is praiseworthy in one respect, has very bad consequences with respect to hygiene because that sense of shame is responsible, directly or indirectly, for the venereal disease problem that is currently afflicting the Annamese. It makes people excessively reticent when discussing sexual matters and also makes them consistently ignore hygienic practices. It perpetuates ignorance about commonplace male-female problems, which affects prostitutes as well. To summarize, it is that sense of shyness that makes Annamese women put up with a disease rather than go to treat it.

That's true, very true.

And so…one, two, three. The School of Sexual Prophylaxis! They must study, they must struggle against their unreasonable shyness, but do not mistakenly think that you do not need to study *that thing* because, as the out-of-touch old folks in our homes say, "You are born like that; no one needs to teach it because everyone knows!" No! There are many paths to *knowledge,* and even if you have already worked as a prostitute, you still must clearly know *it*.

It turns out that our people are inferior in many ways. Thousands of years have already passed, but even the prostitutes don't know how to properly work as prostitutes!

The students include both women with papers and those working clandestinely. They sit here and there, some forty people in all. In the group of girls "without papers yet," there is an unemployed servant, a dim-witted country girl, a girl from a sugar cane shop that believed too much in a boy from a seedy hotel. Among the girls who "have papers" is a girl with a disease who has been confined in the Dispensary and some from outside who are disease-free and have come in response to an announcement for the classes. A strange scene. A strange mix: the coarse, undersized garments of the Dispensary next to the Lemur tunics or the 1937-style overcoats. Pallid complexions next to modern faces with eyes ringed in black, eyebrows that run in opposite directions, and heart-shaped lips.…Lazy students, or thick students, are for the most part girls working clandestinely, who have yet to understand their occupation and are illiterate. Those who learn the lessons by heart, who are the most intelligent and talented in the class, are those with papers, who have already had free-spending lovers, who have wallowed in prostitution for years. Regardless of whether they are skilled or dumb, all of the women must come to class for the examination session.

The teacher, Mrs. Nguyễn Thị Nghĩa, has happily cooperated with the Committee for the Elimination of Venereal Diseases in this very difficult undertaking.

First the devil; second, ghosts; third, students.

But the students are prostitutes. What a chaotic group!

Dear readers, try to imagine seeing a horde of people, "children of whose house" nobody knows, of all ages, of all abilities. If they are stupid, it causes you grief; if they are sly, it kills you because they often feel sorry for themselves and are often filled with indignation. There have been times when they have joined together, for reasons that were unclear, to strike their French sewing teacher. They lie and cheat like demons. They are obedient one minute and then insult their teacher the next, turning in a flash. They study, and study to be prostitutes, but they can spring up during class if their teacher by chance speaks of *working as a prostitute* or *prostitution.*

Therefore, right after she had taken the position and walked into this odd classroom for the first time, Mrs. Nghĩa, with two rows of ivory-like teeth, a white blouse, and a white cap with a red cross on it—a poetic vision like the movie character who comforted wounded soldiers in World War I— immediately had to make concessions to the students. Instead of the teacher entering to students who stand up and fold their arms in one motion, here was a teacher who had to greet the students first.

"Hello, older sisters! The government has just opened this school. Its goal is to teach all of you hygienic methods and other things you need to know to keep yourselves healthy so you can avoid cutting your lives short because an occupation like yours can be very damaging to one's health...."[4]

The teacher had only managed to say that when, from the last row of chairs, a girl with a stuck-up look immediately stood up. Her name was Tâm Thị Dã Mận. One has to be of the "brothel world," and an "older brother" or "older sister" there as well, to have a strange first and last name like that. She arrogantly pursed her lips and spoke for all. "All of us, because we know nothing of sifting or winnowing, we had to stumble into this 'metropolitan flower garden' and have worked in this occupation, so if I still must study something, I suppose I can hope for something more?"

Immediately an uproar arose from the whole group showing its support for the "leader." But Mrs. Nghĩa was calm. "No! Older sisters, you should not talk like that. It's not just you; everyone must know hygienic methods. As for venereal diseases, it's not just you who have them. There are many times when wholesome married couples can get one, simply because they do not understand what hygiene is. That is why the city opened this school, to teach all of you the ways to avoid diseases in your work. All of you should take a look at how much money the government has given; it has spent a very large amount of money in order to protect your health, just like this.... Does that show hatred or scorn for you? We should think seriously about that and see!"

The teacher's words were very calm, very measured. The speaker had made the "masses" throw over their opinions in one stroke. The brothel women had heard it.... The teacher then picked up "The Ballad of Eros" for practice and said, "If someone wanted people to clearly understand their occupation, a Vietnamese poet would compose several verses for them to memorize; then those people would clearly understand the things they needed to do...."

A poem?

Eyes opened wide; mouths opened like the letter O. Oh, in that case it might be fun. Among the clandestine prostitutes there were several from the countryside who had not yet forgotten the lines of doggerel they had sweetly sung behind the green bamboo hedge at transplanting and harvest time.

> Life has eating, drinking, fun, and laughter.
> Carousing, betel, smoking, gambling; isn't that enough?

That is truly great! The teacher read on.... But when the Muse taught about the methods a prostitute must use to examine a client for disease, all of the girls got into a stir.... One girl said loudly and clearly: "Shameful! Shameful!"

The teacher stopped, simultaneously surprised and perplexed. Another student protested. "This time, the government has gone too far; the brothels of Hanoi will all shut down! That's too much; everyone will leave Hanoi! What are we doing studying something so shameful!"

So the shy character of the brothel has come to this? Among these forty people, how many of them, because of this senseless shyness, must carry papers? It's true, because if they knew how to avoid diseases before they were arrested, even though they had already sold their bodies four times, the Bạch My spirit would not have the right to inscribe their names in the Book of Sorrows if the "duck's bill" did not find gonorrhea or syphilis germs. The teacher therefore had to calmly explain again to clarify everything from beginning to end:

> No! Don't think that that is something to be embarrassed about. All of us here who study to be nurses must also know this! If our superiors tell us to examine a man for disease, we still have to perform that medical procedure, do you hear me? In life, you shouldn't think that something is bad; the truth

is there is nothing that is bad. What is bad is ignorance, the thing that lets a disease pass from another's body into one's own! I am not saying that only women working in your occupation need to know the things talked about in the hygiene poem. I am talking directly about honest women who, because they are ignorant, let their husbands go out and carouse and bring diseases back to them. That is something to be embarrassed about, and it is also damaging to their children, damaging to the race. All of you should try to study; don't resist it. The government did not introduce this class with the aim of humiliating you, but with the aim of preserving your health, saving you from dying young, so that in the future you can find a husband and never have to worry about having children!

A few girls broke into skeptical smiles. Another girl with a different idea was somewhat concerned that the teacher's words were an ironic taunt. She spoke in a drawn-out manner. "Madam, you are exaggerating; but for all of us girls here, excuse me, Madam, is there any 'fucking' hope for us?"
There it is, teacher.
There it is, student.

◆◆◆

When I stepped into the classroom, the students were singing.

> Flowing clear water washes away dirty things;
> Fragrant, foamy soap can fully clean everything;
> The client has already finished the first part;
> Don't play further or bad things will come later.
> Careless inattention is the same as giving up;
> You shouldn't blame your disease on others;
> You must treat it quickly to cure it quickly.

They stopped for a minute to turn around and look at me; then all of the girls again sang in resounding unison. The concluding part had an air of optimism that was extraordinarily nice.

> A fortunate life has comfortable days
> Beauty and talent won't let you down!

I had to suppress a smile, seeing that the author of "The Ballad of Eros" wanted to use that literary style to create the fantasy that the world was not a painful place, to flatter and caress the common person's mind, the mind of the brothel, which because it is of the brothel, alas!, is that of the common people and is easily moved by cheap sentiments. *"Beauty and talent won't let you down!"* That is a nice phrase that makes the brothel women forget the Dispensary, the laws that restrict prostitution, the officers of the "Girls' Squad," the "duck's bill"....

Nurse Nghĩa came down from the dais and softly spoke to me. "I think that this might be the last time you will come here. Did you know? The press has given the patients here a difficult time. Perhaps they complained to the chief supervisor so that she would ask the director, the mayor, to no longer allow you to come in. They have complained that they are really miserable and have already been thoroughly humiliated, but the people above still let journalists come in to find stories, to slander them as prostitutes, to speak badly of them, to stare at them as if they were a bunch of tigers, panthers, pythons, and snakes in a zoo. It is really hard for them to take. I am certain that in the near future the officials will take this request into consideration and you will definitely not be given further permission to enter. Isn't that right?"

"Madam, they have misunderstood. If the journalist's occupation is to only say bad things, then I would think that the people who focus on reforming society—the legislators, the politicians—they only say bad things too? But that's all right; if it has come to that, I will leave. I asked to come in this time only because at a minimum I needed to be here to find out a couple of things, that's all. Would you be ready to tell me your impressions from carrying out your duties here?"

She looked pleased. "I have many impressions, Sir. When the director called to offer me this job, I was terribly worried. I clearly recalled the wearisome and disagreeable duties of teachers, who have to deal with the mischievousness, the wickedness, the unruliness of male and female students. Yet who do I teach and where? In the Dispensaire! To the *demi-mondaines!* It truly is a strange school, the most bizarre in Indochina, if not the most bizarre in the whole world. I thought about it for a long time because all of the other male and female teachers follow the old procedures, yet the programs the government had outlined did require teaching. If in the past there were impudent students, the ruler was ready at hand, as were the ways to make them kneel, to punish them. But when the students are *demi-mondaines,* as for being bad, what is worse than having the misfortune of working as a prostitute? As for being scared, what's scarier than being held in the Dispensary? So I asked, should I punish them? Is there anything they are still afraid of? It is truly dangerous. As such, I had to accept this job because thanks to my profession, I understood the scourge of venereal disease more clearly than most. Teaching here, the director has said, is not just a way to earn money; it is a social obligation too."

"Madam, beyond the lessons for practicing hygiene, I have been very interested in one section of the program, the 'Introduction to the Status of Women in Society and the Prostitution Trade.' That is something worth knowing. Therefore, how do you teach that lesson? Do you admonish them to abandon prostitution? To turn a new leaf?"

At this point, Mrs. Nghĩa stopped me with a wave of the hand and said softly: "In the program, though it is briefly stated as such, when it is taught, it is completely different. The dangerous point is that although they are prostitutes, I can never use that language. They are a class of people that are already held in great contempt by society, to the extent that the government has to be cautious, for fear of hurting their pride, for fear that they will feel sorry for themselves. The lesson therefore is only some stories about the ways of the world, and in that I bring in some personal experiences to talk indirectly about the life of the *demi-monde* and family happiness. Everything comes back to a hygienic goal. I have had to bring in the 'princesses' of the prostitution trade, the practitioners of the occupation of marrying Frenchmen (Mrs. Nghĩa was speaking of those women whose great renown we know very well, but I will not go into that because in this life there are still people with more than enough wickedness to drag me into court),[5] the upper-class prostitutes, to come and speak so my students will listen; I tell them that these people, because they know about hygiene and how to preserve their beauty, are respected by the officials and therefore they have wealth and influence. That's how it is. Beyond that, I sometimes talk about getting married, a woman's responsibilities in taking care of the home, family happiness, faithfulness, about not going back to their old ways, etc. Please Sir, do not think that my students are perhaps the most 'conservative' among all women! They have already been damaged by the ideologies of pursuing pleasure, of liberation and equal rights, so when I talk like an old-fashioned moralist, they listen with great admiration."

I turned around and looked at a girl with short, curly hair who was wearing a modern top with a turned-down collar that greatly lacked artistic merit and against whose stomach rested a small purse. She was sitting biting her fingernails and lifted her eyes to look at us. The teacher immediately spoke. "There, don't! Don't judge a book by its cover! Their occupation forces them to dress like that. In truth, they are already very fed up with those modern things."

"Madam, I tremble for all of the 'romantic' women who today are enamored of those modern things, yet in the future they will end up sitting in here, like that…."

The Dispensary teacher smiled faintly and shrugged her shoulders. "That's it! That is the vicious circle. That is…what do you call it?…the cost of progress!"

She stopped for a moment, then continued. "In here, the teacher lags behind the students…. To avert their indignation, many times I have had to sacrifice even myself to explain things to them. I must use myself as an example; otherwise I fear that I will hurt the pride of my female students, the *demi-mondaines*. I will do anything to teach them!"

"Madam, can you do your work so I can see it with my own eyes for a minute, please?"

She sat down on her chair and gently called out. "OK, let's read the lesson! Miss…. Where is Miss Lan? In the last session she hadn't learned the lesson yet, no?"

In the third row of seats, next to a woman in a Lemur tunic, was a girl of about sixteen (all the same, the government must list her as eighteen).[6] Her short, French-styled hair was disheveled, quite dirty, and very ugly. Her face was pudgy and an unhealthy pale. She stood up, folded her arms across her chest, and spoke, at times falteringly, at times fluently, as if she were a parrot. "One adage states: Cleanliness is an excellent doctor. That is very true. It is true that a doctor can only treat a disease, yet cleanliness makes it so that we do not get any diseases. Isn't that better, because if you don't get a disease, then you can avoid painful injections and medicines that are hard to swallow."

The teacher explained. "OK! That was very good! You are a good student! Come up here!"

The student went up to the dais.

"Cleanliness of the genital organs!"

The student read a long passage, sometimes smoothly, sometimes haltingly. She did all right with the theoretical part. When it came to the practical part, the part where she stood before the table that had the hygienic implements and the jars of medicines, she mumbled in confusion, unsure of how to pull off the trick. The teacher immediately grasped the student's hand and weakly struck it a few times against her shoulder, as if she were joking, with a face full of rage.

The student covered her smile, because it didn't hurt. But then two or three other students ran up! They shoved the dim-witted student's head down and at the same time reproachfully said, "You idiot! This kills by chopping, this kills by lopping! There's only one thing like it, but you never remember it, so the teacher's throat is hoarse and her mouth is tired!"

Mrs. Nghĩa turned back to me and explained. "That, Sir, is my punishment policy."

In the strange classroom, the students go after each other every time the teacher needs to punish them.

◆◆◆

The teacher carried on further: "We should not think that women in the Dispensary work only for the rough soldiery, for the lower-class laborers. Westerners' opinions about love are very different from those of our people. Our people don't desire the Dispensary women; they think they are worthless. But Westerners hold that having a Dispensary girlfriend is a great advantage from a hygienic perspective! So we should not be surprised when we see a few Dispensary girls who have papers to work independently; who have a house, a small, private car; who are the lovers of high officials and who go dye their hair on Paul Bert Street for sixteen piasters per session!"[7]

"Madam, certainly those girls are not the students who are difficult to teach?"

"That's exactly it! A few 'upper-class' women like that are sometimes more knowledgeable about hygiene problems than even the teacher! But their number is very small. Most of the girls are thick to the point that, as the saying goes, 'they can't wipe their own noses,' so would you say that it makes life difficult for me? It is true that prostitution is a dangerous occupation! If you turn and look behind you, you will know."

I was startled and turned to look behind me....

Be Advised!

The Commandant, commander of the Hanoi region, and the Mayor remind the people who enter this house to remember the following:

All of the women here may refuse to receive a client, for whatever reason. They do not have to clearly state why if they do not want to.

They have the special right to examine the men who come here. Any men who coerce them will be severely punished.

Signed,
THE COMMANDANT

There are times late at night when gangs of white and black soldiers, slob-bering drunk, go into the brothels and smash up the furniture, hit the girls, and force the unwilling to have sex. The Dispensary teacher has to clearly explain that when there is an emergency, the girls must point to those posters (which are already pasted up in all of the brothels), or if that doesn't work, then immediately call the police, for they cannot have sex with drunken soldiers.

Thus there are times when the doctor performs a medical examination and finds a woman with bruises all over her body.

The clash of the Bạch My and Lưu Linh spirits came when the govern-ment had yet to allow the placement of those posters in the brothels.[8] But when the doctor inquired about the cause, a nonsensical timidity made an injured woman falsely claim, "Sir, I slipped and fell down the stairs!"

I doffed my hat to say farewell to the Dispensary teacher.

The women of the Dispensary stayed in their seats when I respectfully said farewell and went out.

10

The Authorities' Perspective

Can we describe the Dispensary as a charitable facility for courtesans and absolutely never touch upon the prostitution problem? People have already written a great deal about this problem. Thus, just as with the contemporary venereal disease situation, no matter how much is written, there is never a fear of writing too much, and no matter how much is spoken, it is still not enough.

For a journalist who wants to do a *reportage* on prostitution, it is necessary to go out carousing, to go scrounging around for prostitutes in all of the out-of-the-way places. But our ethics do not allow for such activities, even though they are duties that our profession forces upon us. For that reason as well, the task of "investigative interviewing" is regarded as a pretext for carousing, and the relating of those matters in a newspaper has been derided by some as pandering to the corrupt, perverted, obscene, etc. . . . I think this way because I remember the unfortunate things that happened to Việt Sinh when he published his *reportage Hanoi at Night (Hà Nội Ban Đêm)* in the newspaper *Phong Hóa* and suffered from the carelessness and malice of several newspapers.[1]

It is definitely true that, to use Dr. Coppin's words, "If you want to eliminate venereal disease, perhaps the best method is to forbid the people of this land from doing anything that will cause others to catch a disease, but the world has yet to discover a way to do that. In humanity's struggle against venereal diseases, ethical encouragement has been a weapon of both good and ill, but it is effective only at a secondary level, and there have been times that, to the contrary, hygienic methods have had greater effectiveness than ethics."[2] That's exactly how it is. It's just like the noisy clamor that came from the bogus or misguided moralists when they learned of the prostitutes' "Ballad of Eros," which is excerpted in this book.

Now this *reportage* has reached the point in the story where it is essential to have a chapter about…"Hanoi at Night" or "Hanoi Sodom," meaning a short section on carousing by the people of the land of "a thousand-year civilization."

But I will not "investigate" all of the seedy hotels, the devil's dens, the out-of-the-way places. It is not necessary to grease the palms of the boys at the seedy hotels or the nighttime rickshaw drivers, just as it is not necessary to work one's way into the hearts of licensed prostitutes, or those who work clandestinely, in order to learn about prostitution's bad practices and corrupt ways or its ruinous consequences. I will conduct an investigation only from the written works that discuss that problem.…

The authorities' perspective, I want to say, is that of all of the men who have had the responsibility of protecting the races, both French and Vietnamese, such as Coppin, Joyeux, Le Roy des Barres, etc.

In the past ten or fifteen years, how has the Bạch My spirit run wild in the land of Thăng Long?[3] What types of prostitutes, of which races, have maliciously spread the diseases of Venus among the common people?

The authorities have separated the female prostitutes into two categories: those of the yellow-skinned races and those of the white-skinned race. Those of the yellow-skinned group have been further differentiated as follows:

1. Prostitutes with papers *(soumises).*
2. Clandestine prostitutes *(insoumises).*
3. Singers *(cô đầu, chanteuses).*
4. Dancing girls in the dance halls.
5. Women married to Frenchmen.

The yellow-skinned prostitutes are not exclusively Vietnamese. The number of prostitutes from the nation of the "children of heaven" is rather large.[4] Outside of a few girls who have papers, there are countless others who regard themselves as geishas *(cô đầm tẩu).* They work at the large hotels on Hàng Buồm and Hàng Lọng Streets and receive clients only of their own race.

Fifteen years earlier there were Japanese prostitutes. The playboys still remember these small courtesans with eyes with one fold, most of whom were clean, without disease, and very delightful. Regrettably an imperial decree sent by the Japanese emperor to the consul on the problem of national honor robbed the Indochinese capital of these camellia blossoms from the Land of the Rising Sun. Since then, the word *"mousmés"* has been erased from the police register.[5]

PROSTITUTES WITH PAPERS

Prostitutes with papers are those who have a license and must comply with the laws clearly laid out in the governmental decision of February 3, 1921. They are divided into two categories. Members of one category live together in brothels, meaning the houses with the red numbers, and the others are in private houses. The debauchees describe the latter as "holding private papers." In reality, the red-numbered houses in Hanoi are filthy, damp, putrid holes.

At the time when M. Coppin was in charge of the Dispensary, our society had yet to progress or become civilized. Perhaps because of that, most of the brothel women at that time were old, dirty, repugnant, and scabies-ridden. The majority of these women were Annamese, with a few Sino-Annamese mixed-race women and a few Franco-Annamese mixed-race women.

One sees them at the Dispensary; they are the destitute, all in tatters, unkempt; but at night, dressed in smart clothes, wearing jewelry, a layer of makeup covering the filthy bits, some among them have become tempting, good-looking to the eyes of playboys hazy with alcohol. There are some among that group who still look to be in the bloom of youth: they are the debutantes, who will soon wither.

There are some who dress in strange clothes in the evening, sometimes in the European manner, and rent rickshaws to take them to look for clients; the police close their eyes to this special type of advertising, on the condition that the women do not approach Tràng Tiền Street. According to the information that reached my ears (the words of Mr. Coppin), the madams have the right to charge a high price for this independent way of looking for work; perhaps because of that they have no pimps, the special type of pimp that is present in every form of prostitution we see in Europe.[6]

The brothel world had changed by Dr. Joyeux's time. He confirmed this for us roughly as follows: a new mandarin, a new regime—a new brothel, a new regime. In the latter realm, the old faction had moved aside for the young faction because the older ones had become a minority, and they now only take care of the kitchens in the red-numbered houses.

In addition to the two hundred girls who comply with the prostitution law, the number who have fled is between three to six hundred. They flee from the Dispensary. A large number of women are able to flee because the Police des Moeurs in the different provinces do not work together. To give an example, a prostitute in Hanoi has papers, but when she catches a disease, she knows she cannot avoid being confined for a time in the Dispensary, so she hastily flees to Haiphong, where she goes to an affiliated house of prostitution and "works" as a clandestine prostitute. The authorities are not given any information about this, the Girls' Squad in Haiphong is understaffed or helpless, so the woman who fled can work freely and spread venereal disease. There are times when a girl who flees only goes to a clandestine brothel or a seedy hotel next to her old red-numbered house. The Girls' Squad does not have the right to enter and search, so the girl is completely safe. That point sounds contradictory, but that's the reality of it.

CLANDESTINE PROSTITUTES

This group includes people from all classes of Vietnamese society, but the majority come from the lower classes. They start this job from a very young age—twelve, thirteen years old. Although making a truly accurate estimate of their number is difficult, it is said to be around five or six thousand. The Sûreté certified (many years back) that there were more than three thousand. Examinations of these women who have been arrested show that 92 percent have a disease.

Clandestine prostitutes are divided into two groups:

1. Professionals.
2. Temporaries who work as prostitutes for a short time.

The professionals sell their bodies in clandestine brothels. The Girls' Squad knows these houses well, but it does not have the right to go in and make arrests. Houses of prostitution of this style have Franco-Annamese mixed-race girls and sometimes even real French women. French debauchees go to these houses, usually because they are taken there by rickshaw drivers. Beyond that, there are cases when these women are in the red-numbered houses or in the clandestine "branch offices" of red-numbered houses. Official brothels with a license usually have a large number of clandestine brothels, wherein the prostitutes avoid taxes and all of the aggravations that the authorities create for them. The madams can also move around large numbers of girls when business is going well or have them easily evade arrest in dangerous times.

The opium dens also serve the prostitution trade because in those places people have assignations and flirt, so the courtesans can smoke opium and *work* at the same time.

At the inns and seedy hotels, whether the proprietor is Annamese or French, the boys work as intermediaries, and the playboys and prostitutes are at ease because they are not afraid that the police will give them trouble.

Clandestine prostitutes also have private houses. This group includes the comfortably off girls who have the money to rent a private house.

With regard to the women who work as prostitutes for a short time because of poverty, Dr. Joyeux has clearly stated that this is the group of corrupted women who already have an occupation or some position in society, but they have slid into depravity because they want to make money so they can conceal from their families that they have lost money gambling or because they crave a piece of jewelry or want to buy some frivolous item. As in other places, some of these women ultimately become professional prostitutes.

At this point, we need to acknowledge a criticism made by Dr. Le Roy des Barres that makes one feel a little ashamed about Vietnamese society:

> We must be aware of the special mentality of the group of women who work to recruit girls, who prowl around girls' schools, and, after they have promised money and jewelry to poor female students, push some of them into prostitution. The families of those girls usually close their eyes and ignore it if the daughter can earn a little money to supplement family expenses and if everything can be kept secret.
>
> Moreover, the increase in the number of inns and shady rooms for rent, where people post prices by the hour, by the half day, and for the whole day on the seedy hotel door—are they not enough to show us how clandestine prostitution has progressed?[7]

Oh, that's terrible! That is not only worth complaining about from an ethical perspective. It is from a social perspective too! This society, it is true, is vile and wretched in the extreme. Poverty, material squalor, just like spiritual squalor.

The military doctor, Guillemet (*médicin-major* of the Ninth Colonial), had to write the following bitter lines:

> In a country where flesh is offered for the most modest prices, the temptation begins at the garrison's main entrance, near the soldiers guarding the entrance; that temptation is spoken of on the street, on empty streets, just as it is in the crooked drinking establishments or in the brothels. We must recognize that among the total number of soldiers who go out and return to the camp between approximately 9:00 and 11:00 p.m., there are very many

who have fallen into a situation in which they must worry about having a venereal disease.[8]

Then there is Mr. Abadie-Bayro, also a military doctor, who explained that "social wound" in even more dismal terms:

....If I have any equivalent hopes for the Girls' Squad that are not completely useless, then, to the contrary, I believe that that service will assist us
with many tasks. Every time I meet women on Cửa Đông Street, they stand
leaning against trees with a manner that we cannot fail to understand, or
they sit in a long line of ten or fifteen people, underneath the shelters around
the garrison's level walls. Chasing them away is a task that is beneficial and
easy. Among that group of people, I have seen women of all ages, with ragged
and tattered clothing, terrifying numbers of lice, and on their faces and bodies are the indisputable markings of syphilis. It is easy to feel sympathy for
them, for the way they evaluate themselves, as they sell themselves so cheaply
that they no longer need to fear any competition at a lower price. On Mã
Mây Street people rent out a small room with one woman for two hào. On
Đường Thành Street, Cửa Đông, in the deep holes around the garrison or in
the vacant grassy areas adjacent to the train tracks, surrounded by a natural
scene that the Creator has made into a screen, the price is only five xu, or if
haggling reduces it by one or two, then all that is left is three xu. There are
times when people reach the final limit of compromise as well. At present,
in the base hospital, I am treating a young soldier who very seriously con-
fessed to me, with no intention of joking, that in spending one xu, he bought
gonorrhea and a chancre and lay on his back in bed for three weeks. You
don't have the money? People exchange commodities; the proof is in a case
that a doctor related to me in which he had to sign the papers for a terribly
unfortunate woman for free admission to a hospital. She was already several
months pregnant, and all the clothing she had to cover her body was a pair
of pants from a former French soldier that she pulled up high to cover her
breasts![9]

SINGING GIRLS (CÔ ĐẦU)

The singing girls are the *ả đào,* women who have given us happiness in Vạn
Thái, Khâm Thiên, or those who have made us miserable. In writing about
this, I must insert a parenthetical comment to clarify that it is not I myself

who puts them in the prostitution trade! That is the authorities' point of view....I ask the reader to clearly remember that. The authorities have even listed the dancing girls from the dance halls in the prostitution register, not just the singing girls. But enough; let's see what Dr. Coppin has to say about this:

> The *à đào* girls, who previously were the very delightful and high-spirited Egéries in the establishments to which the literati and scholars went in order to find inspiration for their writing, have now gone into decline; the heroic age is over, and we can perhaps now say that it is primarily the *à đào* girls who are the real source of the venereal scourge spreading into upstanding Vietnamese families. It is in the *à đào* establishments in particular that people organize banquets, a place for their close friends, and of course, the wives are at home at the time; because of that, one scene that I have witnessed with my own eyes is that the husband catches a disease and goes home and gives it to his wife, but the wife regards only the husband's extramarital affair as the serious matter and does not care about the disease that her husband gave her.[10]

Then there is Dr. Joyeux shouting about the mandarinate's influence in preserving the honor of the *à đào* women so that they can avoid medical examinations:

> The madams are normally geishas, or bogus *à đào* women, who have sold themselves to men with power or to the nouveau riche, who, because they do not want to take them home, set up businesses for their lovers. The men with authority often interfere, and often get into disputes, whenever the authorities are about to ask the women about improprieties. Apart from that, there are some mandarins who protect them. Because they are outside of the city's land, all of the *à đào* women are under the administrative authority of the Annamese mandarinate. There is a very large number of mandarins who have an interest in these protective activities, either directly or indirectly.[11]

The mandarinate protects the *à đào;* that is very useful for the *à đào* faction. But what about society? How, therefore, does the business of protecting them influence society? Again, the words of Dr. Joyeux:

> I have known of many dramas in families, between husbands and wives, that have been caused by those women! How much strife, how much spiritual corruption in how many people, has been their fault! It is true that it has

become more than commonplace to hear about a clerk who in the past was serious and loyal to his boss but then unexpectedly embezzles money, the reason being those *à đào* women. There are hundreds of young or middle-aged men who embezzle or go broke because of the *à đào*.

We have seen that the vast majority of the *cô đào* houses do not have a girl who can play an instrument or do anything with music, except on Khâm Thiên, in the houses that have a name for having one or two girls with a few humble talents. Therefore, when they are seriously looked at, people have enough evidence to regard those singing establishments as brothels, and they are no more luxurious than the brothels. If we want to be fair, it must be said that the women we meet in the singing houses are better than the courtesans. Usually they are not dirty, common, vulgar like the courtesans. Many girls look very smart, with very elegant clothing.... How unfortunate! With regard to hygiene, these women have not progressed very much; they are still as ignorant as when they first entered the trade. If the bosses have looked after their intellect and taught them how to make themselves up and how to behave as refined people, by contrast they will absolutely never dare touch upon the things they need to know about male-female sexual relations; there is never a single recommendation about hygiene, they do not know what cleanliness is, they never have a single implement that they need for their occupation.[12]

The points recounted here, although they are true, are not enough to make the director of the Municipal Hygiene Service categorize the *à đào* as belonging to the common brothels, even if the "Enemy Number 1" of the *à đào* women concludes it all by saying the following:

For the Annamese, "going to sing" means going out from sundown and visiting various haunts, for a long or short time, until a choice has been made, and then staying there until late at night and then going home or staying until the following morning. The truth is that now there are no longer any *à đào* establishments; in reality they are brothels, dance halls, seedy hotels; from a material or legal perspective, we must say that they are no better than the other locales, such that, according to the meaning established by the authorities, they are "places where people promote, encourage, or condone the prostitution trade." The name "*à đào* house" is used by clients because of their ridiculous snobbishness, by clients with just a few coins and from the lower classes. Except for Khâm Thiên, the prices in the *à đào* neighborhoods are very low, and the competition with the red-numbered houses is fierce. That is true because the prices in the brothels range from twenty cents to one piaster, excluding the entrance fee and gift money for the girl. However, at the bogus singing houses there is another special rate: five or six mandarins can stay for the entire night, to drink, play, eat, etc.—and only have to pay one piaster![13]

There it is. Dr. Joyeux clearly understands how well developed the politesse of the Annamese pleasure seeker is!

DANCING GIRLS

This is a product of Westernization (100 percent, yes!) and the liberation of women. Within our society there is a group of people, those who are superficial and obsessed with new things, who are always howling about it. The result: the Bạch My spirit has acquired a new type of prostitution, just as women have also acquired a new occupation that serves debauchery. On this point, I don't want to argue with the proprietors of the dance halls. I am putting forth the criticisms of the director of the Dispensary regarding this art form, criticism as seen through the eyes of a scientist—and whoever says "scientist" also means "sociologist"—to make those who are fond of the French think about and become aware of how they look down upon us:

> Five years ago there were no "dancing" houses in either Hanoi or its outskirts. At that time, such establishments had no reason to exist, the main reason being that the number of Vietnamese women who knew how to dance was still very small. There were only those women who lived in European milieux or whose families had become Westernized. As such, people regarded it as something special when there was dancing at get-togethers. When seeing those self-important and very "avant-garde" girls wearing the national dress, which bears a small mark of European fashion, while held in the arms of a European or Annamese man and moving their high-heeled feet in time to a Slow Step, Annamese citizens did not know whether they should praise what they saw or regard it as disgraceful. If, from this point of view, public opinion on this matter was in such accord that there was unanimous agreement, we could speculate that there was one thing that we would never be wrong about: that these ways of dancing would never become fashionable; they would always be performed under special circumstances and would never have the ability to spread among the Annamese masses because modern Western dancing demands from a person a hereditary disposi-

tion that, from the distant past, the Annamese people have never had. The Annamese are among those least fond of dancing in the world. It is surprising when we recognize that, in fact, when they want to express collective happiness or fun—and it is the same throughout the country—there has never been collective singing or dancing among the masses. The ways of dancing that accord with the meaning mentioned above [here Dr. Joyeux wants to speak of spirit mediumship], in truth are only ways of performance, posture, rhythmic gesture, that record legendary heritage or religious hopes.[14] Furthermore, the Annamese people, as told in the history books, have also never had a time when they have been happy enough that their gaiety made them want to dance. From another perspective, the Annamese, according to their hereditary disposition, do not dance and have also never demonstrated the qualities suitable for artistic dancing to music; besides, contemporary ways of dancing rely on certain freedoms with regard to customs, and the Annamese cannot tolerate the morals of our ancestors. Second, Western and Eastern music are different to the extent that it bursts our brains and we cannot understand their music, just as their ears can in no way understand ours; because of that, we cannot understand each other, and we can perhaps conclude that they do not feel any innate passion, just as they do not have ready the essential qualities for dancing.

Only a perfunctory visit to a few streets in Hanoi or in the Khâm Thiên area, however, is enough to show us that the above observations are completely invalid. Or is it that the method of reasoning, because it did not thoroughly examine psychological factors, is therefore mistaken? No! It is because it omitted the unusual ease of the Annamese in imitating others in order to keep up with the times, especially when they have been pressured by the strong desire to be seen in their finery—that is, because of a spirit of arrogance, of ostentation. Through the encouragement of the French government (in policies of closeness, cooperation, Franco-Viet harmony, total Western education, etc.), a wave of Europeanization has recently risen among the youth and spilled over into the masses. And like a tidal wave (though it is only a facade), it has in a few families overturned the ancestral altar and taken along with it the ancient morals and customs. The youth therefore fervently display their intoxication with Europeanization and grow fanatical toward that new religion! There is nothing European that is not worth studying, noting, copying, assimilating. It is primarily because of this moral and spiritual revolution that, in spite of encountering obstacles, these dancing arts have sprouted and blossomed in an incredibly rapid manner.

It was not long until the movement, which spread slowly for a bit, had conquered all parts of the city and given the *à đào* neighborhoods a new look. In the beginning the Khâm Thiên neighborhood was the aristocratic area for the brothels and had the best dance establishments; other areas in the outskirts are following that movement slowly and with difficulty because the mandarins in those areas did not belong to the elite.

Naturally, the dance halls in the outskirts can survive only next to the *à đào* establishments. The schools for teaching Western dance, which have been established by unemployed youth who have taken the innovative step of opening them, produce the "female cavalry."[15]

Their success is well worth describing. In order to retain clients, the madams send a few girls to study. They purchase a gramophone and the newest records. Seeing that they are getting good results, a few people set up dancing rooms that have a bar for selling the newest drinks as in Europe. Then more spacious establishments spring up with only that goal in mind. At the dance schools the students flood in, especially during these times of economic difficulties since someone working as a taxi girl only half time can earn money incredibly easily! The dance halls hire the taxi girls for high wages (from 15 to 30 piasters to dance for a few hours every night). At the dance halls, whether they sell alcohol or not, and at the *à đào* establishments, the pleasure seekers jostle with each other, especially the progressive youth, who consider European dancing a badge of honor that shows their liberation and high status. Thus, in those neighborhoods, we have started to see that Europeans, who are not skilled in Annamese language or customs, have found a way to interact with local young women. The *à đào* establishments that have a dance floor also have a lot of customers, even though they have slowly lost their previous character. The madams of the establishments without dance floors have acquired the habit of sending their most appealing girls to the other places to bring back guests. This is one defining feature regarding the nature of "houses of prostitution" that the *à đào* establishments in the singing community have brought upon themselves. The dancing girls, with their faces carefully made up in the newest ways and their very elaborate dress, have become the most elevated class, and the French bourgeoisie, with their money for play ready at hand, are always looking for them."[16]

Speaking of contemporary ways while saying annoying things about us *(the authorities)* [continue]:

It is undeniable that with the new tendency the transformation of prostitution makes the situation more desperate for those involved, just as the sphere of their activities increases. Instead of girls working as *ả đào* only to furnish busy people with a few moments of spiritual diversion, the shocking method of getting rich in the dancing trade is enough to confirm for us that they no longer maintain the older meaning and that with the *ả đào*, Western dancing is only a method for using an artistic motive to sell themselves more easily and for a higher price. The evidence shows that their dancing is not for even the smallest aesthetic reason, and that is because there is not a girl among them who has the essential artistic qualities to perform the genuine art of Terpsichore because the truth is that they were not born into that art by the Creator. That does not apply to girls who dance properly but to those who know how to guide men in teaching them to dance. For those reasons, dancing in these locations has the consequence of being very convenient for the prostitution trade. It is primarily due to dancing, a product of Europeanization, that we must accept the bane (truly the proper way of things in this world, with their advantages and disadvantages) of how many venereal disease germs are spreading even to Europeans. It is true that in the past European soldiers only infrequently went to the *ả đào* neighborhoods because they were not here long enough to learn the Annamese language and customs. Today, a new language has recently emerged. Not only do we see European soldiers in the afternoon hunting for a good catch, but we also run into them happily arm in arm with their "girls" because they have found themselves with "girlfriends" in an atmosphere they enjoy. From this unique perspective, the soldiers are not incorporated into the important group of pleasure seekers in those neighborhoods because although they do go there, the *ả đào* neighborhoods still preserve a lot of the local character that European soldiers have yet to fully grasp. From a different perspective, the *ả đào* neighborhoods are very important for the public health situation of the army because more and more every day the soldiers are blinded by the charms of the *ả đào* girls, so they must go to those places to take temporary wives who are rarely faithful and for whom they will rent houses near the base.[17]

WOMEN MARRIED TO FRENCHMEN *(ME TÂY)*

These women can also—of course!—be classified as clandestine prostitutes. Here we can follow the explanation of Dr. Coppin:

> The "girl friends," *congai (con gái),* or the "Western women" [*cô tây*] are the Annamese women living as husband and wife with Europeans![18] They

constitute a distinct class, living outside of the restrictions of Vietnamese society and suffering from society's scorn (except when they have become wealthy, which has happened with a few clever women when they have gotten older). The majority of this type are originally from lower-class homes, and it is only because of money that they live with Europeans, and they hold that fidelity is not something that must be onerous and...worrisome for them. A very large number of *me tây* often get extra money by going to clients when the "husbands" are not at home or are not keeping an eye on them, or they have extramarital relations with one or more lucky male friends of their own race, who on many occasions benefit from the largesse of these women. We can perhaps believe that most of the latter apprentice pimps are not disease-free, from a venereal disease perspective. As for the "husband" being disease-free or not, that is not something that is necessary to know because maybe he is afflicted with chronic venereal disease. Supposing, therefore, that he is reinfected with a disease; no one really knows if a person outside of the family transmitted it or not. There is also a relatively large number of these women whose princely husbands have returned to France, but they still send money to them, primarily to care for their children, but usually they do not send enough. Among these people the scourge of a horrible obsession with gambling is often the reason for their haphazard romances.[19]

Those are the final lines in the list of prostitutes, official or clandestine, belonging to the yellow-skinned races in the capital city Thăng Long. But the city of Thăng Long of the Lê kings is now Hanoi, under the regime of the empire of the Third French Republic. There, the yellow-skinned "people" *(hommes jaunes)* live alongside the "white gods" *(dieux blancs)*.

Thus there are even white-skinned women among the ranks of prostitutes. And standing at the fore of this group are several Franco-Vietnamese mixed-race women.

FRANCO-VIETNAMESE MIXED-RACE WOMEN (ĐẦM LAI)

Here again the words of Dr. Coppin on the chaotic unions of Franco-Vietnamese mandarin daughters.

In Hanoi there is already a large number of these girls, and not all of them can find work or marry a proper husband. It is saddening when we realize that the educational methods used in the religious schools cannot change in the slightest the fragile moral character that is often seen in people of two races. These young women without parents, as I well know, are not worth trying to completely sort out, and the charitable associations cannot do everything for them, yet I also know that a number of these women, because of their ignorance, spread the venereal poison among the European and Annamese masses. The Sûreté here has some rather important reports on the activities of some mixed-race women, but I must say here that a great deal of influence has been exerted by French people who have interfered on behalf of these women so that they need not worry about anything.[20]

For Dr. Joyeux, the exposition of that sad situation is even clearer. He was not afraid that his "honest words" would be "shocking to hear"! In 1930 he had already said the following:

This is a problem that is difficult to speak about. . . . This group brings to the mixed-race people the bad points of both races brought together as one; others are very indignant every time they hear some insinuation that does not sound amusing to their ears. We do not pay attention to these contradictory viewpoints because we pay attention only to those things that are related to the venereal scourge. The words of Dr. Coppin, alas!, still capture the reality: "In Hanoi there is already a large number of these girls, and not all of them can find work or marry a proper husband." They suffer from neglect by others, they are despised by others; they despise others, they envy others; there is nothing worth being surprised about if there are many women who allow themselves to be dragged into prostitution. Very few "have papers." Only three women do (this figure is from 1930).

Other women, who are more numerous, work as clandestine prostitutes in their homes—this is also rare—or in the big hotels to which the boys or rickshaw drivers bring them or often in the seedy hotels, meeting houses, or opium dens.[21]

Most of the women who encounter misfortune have *boyfriends* with whom they live as husband and wife because they must do this in an attempt to get a real marriage or at least to live a luxurious life relative to the Europeans, who make these women think that in doing so, they can be liberated from their mixed Annamese blood. Sometimes they can also find a husband, but most of those are French functionaries who, when they return to France, either abandon them or say farewell with many sweet words and very little money, and as such they must find *someone* who will maintain them in the happy situation they cannot leave behind. However, one thing is more or less true, and that is that from a venereal point of view, the mixed-race women have created a connection that is expanding every day, and the time has come when we must have an appropriate method to protect against them and control them.[22]

Messieurs Coppin and Joyeux were speaking in the distant past. The problem of young mixed-race women has at present become more difficult, or it's no longer difficult at all, because at one time the Protectorate government lacked the capacity to properly care for some of the Franco-Vietnamese women. These women imperiled the ability of the conquering race in a colonized land to maintain its prestige because many of the Franco-Vietnamese women dressed like the indigenous prostitutes and were confused with the native population. They also had foul mouths and used sexual references to curse others, just like authentic Vietnamese women!

FRENCH WOMEN (ĐẦM THẬT)

These are 100 percent Western women. We should not be surprised or hesitant to talk about this because prostitution is a wound on all humanity.

On this topic, Mr. Coppin was economical with his words. He wrote only one line: "A few Western women, either married or unmarried, undoubtedly constitute a contagious group: we do not need to say much…."[23] But if we want to thoroughly understand this matter, let's look at the proclamations of Dr. Joyeux:

Prostitution by European women in Hanoi, which has yet to have the same significance as in Saigon, involves only a few women. In the past this trade was virtually monopolized by a few women from Valaques, as was clearly stated in the decision of January 1, 1906, and in the police regulation of May 18, 1915. These women, who originally came from Central Europe, came here during the French occupation of Vietnam and opened cafés in which the back areas were used for prostitution. Nearly all of these women were deported around 1919. However, there are two people who still remain, but they do not engage in prostitution because of their advanced age.

At present there are no longer any European women with papers. There is only one elderly woman whose name remains in the register of the Police des Moeurs, but she has not gone to the Dispensary for a sanitary visit since

1923; she is the proprietor of a café where married European women or mixed-race women go to meet their clients.

But we should not be too hasty in feeling happy about the morals of our countrymen (this is what the French say) because those morals are only as the government wants to report them. For very many reasons, right or wrong, Tonkin strenuously avoids forcing even one French prostitute to hold papers. Saigon, a city that is not all that different from Hanoi, has up to 150 French prostitutes who are obliged to comply with the laws that regulate prostitution. But the government has laws that forbid French prostitutes from Saigon from setting foot in Haiphong. Thus, in Tonkin there are no official French prostitutes, but there are clandestine prostitutes. To be precise, their number is not very great. Yet professional French prostitutes are usually protected by some job, business, playboy, or influential patron, to such an extent that by simply seeing their faces, the Police des Moeurs or the regular police are stricken with terror, so they think it is better to close their eyes and ignore them than to create major complications. Most of the French prostitutes are proprietors of opium dens, places for assignations, that are usually very attractively decorated and very popular, both for people (true French women and mixed-race women) and for venereal disease germs.

As for the occasional prostitutes, this group is quite numerous: women who have husbands but like to live a luxurious life and are married to officials with small salaries; unmarried women struggling against poverty; young girls drawn to corrupt amusements.... We should say what Coppin said: "We do not need to say much." The French and Annamese hotels, especially the Hotel Nagasaki, have hidden within them who knows how many secrets![24]

◆◆◆

There, we have in one pass reviewed all of the artisans in Hanoi's prostitution industry, all of the Dispensary's patients.

Regarding the causes of the prostitution scourge, all of the authorities have condemned the surge of materialism, meaning the Westernization of male and female young people. All of the doctors furrow their brows at the liberated lives of women and complain about the loss of the father's authority in Annamese families. One thing to which it is worth paying a great deal of attention is that all of these men lament the destruction of our ancestral altars. As that bell rings, I would like to cite an example from Dr. Coppin because it sounds funny to our ears and is the most penetrating:

In this country, very profound moral reasons have given rise to the character of the venereal scourge and its expansion.

One day, in Paris, I met a former student of mine and asked him, "Why do you, in your country, not do your utmost to eliminate a scourge that has necessitated failure in the achievement of your legitimate aspirations—that is, the horrifying greed for money that plays a dominant role in all kinds of bribery and dishonest scheming in men and all manner of deterioration in the virtue of women in your society?"

He responded to me, "But those bad practices, which I recognize are there, were in fact brought over to our country by you! Before there was a protectorate, we didn't have those bad practices at all!"

The response was very biased and contrary to the truth because there were corrupt practices that everyone knows about, that have been taking place from the time that Vietnam was under Chinese influence, and today people have quickly forgotten them; however, that response indirectly had one part that was true.

No one denies that living conditions for a large number of people in the country are better than before, especially in the large cities. The progress of European civilization has at the same time brought over its own costs: in its contact with affluence, family morality has loosened, and collapsing along with it are all of the things that are the pillars and foundation of Oriental morality.

Relations between men and women are becoming freer every day, and the status of Annamese women is also changing, with the result that they have power and can do whatever they wish to do; divorces, illicit relationships, are forever increasing, and—something that never existed in the past—scandals caused by passion now fill the front pages of the newspapers every day and occur in the upper classes of society as well.

Except for fathers who still have some authority in their families, there is nothing to prevent the deterioration of customs and morality; common people know nothing of the essence of the morality of Buddhism, Daoism, or Confucianism, just as they do not know that there is Buddhism, Daoism, or Confucianism. Popular religion is only the senseless making of offerings, vulgarity, nonsensical spirit mediumship, within which there has never been the smallest consideration of moral principles; a few of the predilections of the village guardian spirits, as explained by my friend Maspéro, are obscene, thoroughly despicable.[25]

From this point of view, we should take the occasion to note that the spirit of our Gallic ancestors, if it has been the genesis of many of the positive virtues of the French race, has conversely also had a large influence on the perversion of customs and the bitter consequences of those perversions; because of that, the indecent atmosphere of the French colonies runs counter to the solemn moral atmosphere of the English colonies.

But the popular spirit of the Annamese is perhaps very much in accord with the spirit of the Gauls on this point. Annamese literature often has erotic stories (Kim Văn Kiều and all of the folk songs, proverbs, paired singing in the countryside). The Annamese people like making vulgar jokes, and their everyday cursing is in no way less biting than the curses of Arabs or Persians (see the studies of Chéon and others discussing the lower-class language of Annam). There is a large store of oral sayings that speaks of these matters in an exceedingly free manner, and among the people there is no one who has not mastered them; even the young know them, and those things have a close correlation with the playful voice of our Rabelais; who is surprised when they find in Annam's *Tiếu Lâm* that there are stories that are similar to those of Béroalde de Verville?[26]

For many different reasons, and other short-sighted reasons that I will explain, venereal diseases, which usually go along with male and female sexual relations like a shadow follows a person, have in this country found a soil that seems to have been prepared to greet venereal disease germs.[27]

Is it like that? As we have seen, the authorities have carefully researched the prostitution problem here. Be it a director of the Dispensary or a doctor from private practice or from the military, they have all been in agreement, and whenever they have spoken, they have said that the evidence is clear, and they have correctly described the facts. If the government with its firm resolve still cannot complete the task of eliminating prostitution, it is because humanity cannot live without prostitution!

Now that we know that, we should learn about the feelings of courtesans when they started their careers in the proper manner—that is, the moment they started to ... hold papers.

11

Holding Papers

The women of the Dispensary live the lives of the "closed gates and high-walled women's apartments," like the secluded young women of high-born nobility.... They had asked the administration to prevent me from entering the Dispensary! I can no longer go where they are! Luckily I thought of a way around this: if it has come to this, then I can probably arrange it so that they must come to where I am! And it is this fact that distinguishes them from other secluded young women.

Therefore, this evening a boy from the seedy hotel V. L. stared in astonishment when he saw a gentle person, one who almost seemed like a fool, perch on a table and attempt to imitate the eloquent voice of an authentic playboy in order to issue a frightful order: "Boy, go get me two women from a brothel. It doesn't matter which one, but I want one girl who's old and ugly and another who's still young, who's only been working in the trade for a short time."

I didn't care to look at the boy's face when I said that. Before he left, I could hear his uneven and unsure footsteps behind me. I knew that he had to turn around and take a look at me from the back, some two or three times. He thought I was insane. That was true. After twenty years of experience in his job, this was perhaps the first time he had met a playboy as strange as me.

◆◆◆

Where were the Police des Moeurs?

This seedy hotel, it is true, is part of the inheritance of the clandestine prostitution trade. I was standing in an upstairs corridor and could clearly see six women. They were in a room, and when somebody wanted to stay in that room, a boy herded them into a neighboring room that was in even worse shape. Two times the two doors were thrown wide open, two times the lamplight shone brightly on that flock of sheep. I had already seen a woman with a gauzy black shirt and crimson silk trousers. Another woman was dressed like a silk trader from the countryside. Two other people were dressed like country folk. One woman wore modern clothes, and another was holding a conical hat. She must have been a street peddler. Long live the hotel's old boss! The old guy had all the women he needed: modern, rural, old-fashioned, maids, servants, a "careful" trader; he could probably extend his hospitality to even the most difficult customers.

And the boys will scratch their heads and say to the client, "Yes, Sir, it's quite certain with her. She's a silk trader from Đình Bảng! Oh, she's very careful because on the first time she wants to earn a bit extra...." Or he'll say, "Yes, yes! You wouldn't believe it! She just came from the countryside two days ago. She dresses like a country girl and still doesn't know how to wear shoes!" Or he'll say something like, "Yes, of course! If you want modern, you can get modern! She's from a reputable family...but the price is a little higher. If you give me five piasters, I'll go call her."

After that, the boy will eloquently guarantee dishes that are juicy, certain, careful, and reputable, but he will also note that they are far away, quite far away, on Hàng Trống Street, Chợ Hôm Street, Quán Thánh Street, etc.... The client gives him a few coins for a rickshaw. The boy goes downstairs, lies down and has a nap, or smokes a few pipes of opium, then tells a girl who has been herded into the neighboring room to go upstairs, where he testily demands more rickshaw money if he wasn't given enough before.

But that is the business of the playboy clients or the officers of the Girls' Squad, and it creates no complications for me.... Now then, "my people" have arrived. I must now go into the room that I rented.

"Oh ho! You really are something!"

It couldn't be denied; this time I'd really gotten full of myself. The boy hadn't cheated me. Here were two authentic women "with papers"! I had already seen one of them, in the Dispensary, during my first visit to their domain. She had seen me too, and she remembered my face. She walked in and immediately said to me, "You are something!"

She continued, calling me "older brother" while calling the boy "uncle":[1] "So it's this guy again! When the boy called for me, I thought it was strange and had no idea why a mandarin would want to do such an over-the-top thing. He's only got himself, but he wants to go up against two! The boy said that the man had also said that the oldest and ugliest should go. That's even stranger! Anyway, you still want to gossip with us so you can put it in your newspaper?"

I didn't respond. I turned my hand toward a chair and said, "Go ahead and sit down!"

I looked at her from head to toe. A blue tunic, threadbare white satin pants, a pair of dancing shoes. On top of those was the kind of face one would never believe was real if one had never walked into a brothel. She wasn't just ugly; she was repulsive to the point of making one nauseous. Two cheeks that looked like rice cakes…a pair of thick lips…two tiny eyes…alas, it's hard to describe! She had a stomach and two thighs that could envelope an average-sized man. And her arms could squeeze that man to death. And then on top of those…powers, there was the bubbly voice and cackling laugh that is unique to brothel women.

The younger girl was much easier to look at! But there was something about her that stops one from feeling pleased with a courtesan, though if we hold her responsible for that, we will get a reputation for being a bit crazy! Nevertheless, in spite of everything, she still looked really good. Imagine the soul of a dim-witted country lass in the body of a brothel girl, wrapped in cheap and worn-out clothing, and you'll get the picture. The two women had something very similar and also something very different. One "inexperienced" face next to the face of another skilled in the trade. And those two types of faces fit with what I wanted.

I said to them, "You two will stay here with me all night, but we are not going to…'play'!"

They looked at each other, surprised. Then, after they had clearly heard what I was saying, the older woman immediately asked me, "If it's like that, then you've got to at least let me smoke some opium, or it'll be too fucking boring. If I don't smoke, how can I stay awake?"

The "inexperienced" girl immediately shouted out, "Oh, that's great!"

I turned around and said to the boy, who at that point was still standing and waiting for instructions outside the room, "Come and get some money and buy me a packet of opium, and then bring an opium set up here!"

Outside it was windy and rainy. Winter had arrived two weeks ago. It was a sad type of night that put people in the mood to talk about their life stories and their worries about the future. Once she started talking, Miss Lành (the name of the older woman) became quite loquacious.[2]

"If you ask, then I've got to answer, but my life isn't really worth talking about! It's only going to seem clichéd! I'm like a ferryboat. Everyone who crosses rides it!"

As I didn't want to hurt a woman's pride (even though she was a brothel worker), I rested my head on her thigh, closed my eyes, and didn't bother her as she smoked and worked the opium.… But seeing that she was wandering too far off the subject, I had to open my eyes wide in order to put a stop to that inspiring tale.

"All right! I told you to tell me about the time when you started to hold papers. Come on! What was it like?"

"Ah! OK! I thought you wanted to hear about life in the *demi-monde!* But the opium comes first; otherwise I'll be angry and demand to leave right now!"

After I had taken a draw on the pipe, she softly slapped me. Yến lay there calmly resting her head on my shin as she playfully moved a match over the bowl of the pipe.

"Damn! If only we had clients like this every night; what a life! Working in a brothel would be great!"

Lành stared into my eyes and continued in the coddling manner of a courtesan. "Why do you have the kindness of the Buddha, hmm?"

This was the second time I had to remind her to talk about the first time she carried papers. It wasn't an easy thing to do: most prostitutes don't know how to hold a proper conversation; they don't clearly understand the meaning of our everyday sentences. If they speak, they will often use only the kind of language that cannot be found in the *Sino-Vietnamese Dictionary!* But I can explain it as follows.

❖❖❖

Maybe she got into prostitution because she was depraved and lazy. She got into the business very early: fifteen years old. At that time the Dispensary was still in a shrine in the area of the mayor's office that is now the Children's Garden.

From the time she was very young, she had neither a mother nor a father. How did she live? That is a secret. When she was fourteen, she was still pouring water into cricket nests, running around the trunks of trees to catch cicadas that hadn't shed their skins, or grabbing rocks and pieces of wood and throwing them into the sapindus and tamarind trees. She caught the crickets to cook and eat and the cicadas to sell for half a xu each. She would eat the soap nuts from the sapindus trees or the tamarind or sell them to buy rice. People scornfully said of her, "A girl…hardly; she's like a boy! She's obviously a slut!" She did those things to stay alive, so she was stunned by their reproaches. Anyway, she couldn't do that anymore. So she changed jobs. From then on, people saw Lành with a small flat basket that held a few pieces of manioc, a few pomelo sections, a few dozen guava, a small basket of roasted peanuts. Needless to say, she didn't have a permit.[3]

It was a tough job. You can't make anything from it! But then she would see the police, or the people would check for her permit, and on rainy days with strong winds the city's children wouldn't come out and play on the sidewalks. One evening in Paul Bert Square an older Vietnamese soldier bought a few pomelo sections and then told her to come with him. Initially she hesitated and was scared.... But when it came down to it, she was curious. She really wanted to know *what it was like*. Furthermore, her basket was full, and in her pocket she didn't have the money to buy even a measure of rice. That was a powerful reason to make her decide.

Then, the morning after, the soldier gave her three hào! Three copper ten-cent pieces that were still new, shiny, and glittering. She really liked the look of them. Anyway, we shouldn't find fault with the greediness of those of earth's creatures who know how to spend money once they catch the smell of it.

From that point on, when she went to sell pomelo, Lành didn't push away the hands of clients who touched her breasts, and when they whispered in her ear, she didn't shake her head and refuse.

She had an officer from the Girls' Squad take her to the Dispensary at four o'clock in the morning, when she and a young dandy came out of a seedy hotel. The doctor examined her and discovered that she had both syphilis and gonorrhea!

"I had to stay in there for six months before I recovered from the diseases. It was the first time I had been caught, so I didn't need to get papers. But then I had to get papers! I had to ask for papers immediately! They made sure of it! It's like I just told you: going to jail makes prisoners of men; going into the Dispensary makes prisoners of women."

She said that, but no one understood at all what she meant!

"Who is 'they'? What are you trying to say?"

She started sharply, "*They* means the women from the brothels who were being held in the Dispensary to get their diseases treated; who else is there! The old ghosts torment the new ghost, over and over again! The madams likely lacked people, so they told their juniors to force me to get papers. There wasn't a night that they didn't give me a beating like a beating in Central.[4] The men who go to jail are not tormented by the guards at all! It's only the prisoners, imprisoned for life, who have lived there a long time and become the old men of the village, who don't have to be afraid of anything anymore—they are the ones who really torment the 'new soldiers' terribly and mercilessly! The women who are sent to the Dispensary also get that...."

Up to this point Lành had ground her teeth and indignantly remembered this injustice of twenty years ago. She had already tried to show me that the Dispensary of that time was a horrible prison for the courtesans; this was the one that was in the old shrine in the area of the mayor's office.

It was a "house" divided into two compartments. You crossed a small courtyard and entered into a spacious room with large wooden columns that held up transverse beams, each of which was adorned with carvings: dragons, phoenixes, the faces of tigers, and the character for longevity. Inside there were wooden platforms for approximately sixty people to lie on. Usually over one hundred women were put in there, detained in that cramped space, where in the summer it became unbearably hot and in the winter freezing cold. Next to the sleeping room was the examination room, which was as spacious as a nostril. On Tuesdays and Fridays all of the women from Hanoi's brothels had to come in; it was an unusual spectacle. By the end of the examination session, the whole place was covered with red spit from women chewing betel. The girls with clean clothes would put lotus leaves on the seats to keep the seats of their pants clean or to prevent the smearing of filth onto their pants when they sat down. It made one nauseous looking at it.

Every night, one hundred girls, clandestine and with papers, were thrown together in a room that had space for only sixty to lie down; it really made for some hard-to-tell stories. People would insult, hit, scream, and yell at each other. A lot of girls would sing in a very happy way; those were the girls who, because of their troubled situations, had already gone mad or were about to go mad.

So when Lành was almost cured of her diseases, every night there were three women "with papers," all of whom genuinely deserved the fear they inspired, advising her that she should ask for papers.

"Hey, don't worry; having papers is great! There's no need to duck and dive like a thief anymore! We can openly ply our trade. There's nothing to fear from the Girls' Squad anymore!"

"When the director allows you to leave, ask to get papers immediately; then you can come and work at my place. I'll look out for you and teach you so you can really learn how to make money. So tell me, is it yes or no?"

Lành got both gentle persuasion and beatings. There was nothing that those women didn't try. One time the women tore at her genitals, after they had taken a hairpiece and rammed it up her anus! She held out for about three nights, but on the fourth night she got down on the ground and, soaked with tears, said, "I bow down before you; don't hit me anymore! I will definitely ask for papers and will go to your place!"

The women slapped her until she had sworn to it six or seven times.

"You say that, but if you don't do as you say, I'll kill you!"

"If you don't ask for papers, don't expect to survive the next time you come in here!"

"Don't think that once you get out of here you'll never have to come back again!"

Lành kept bowing her head before them; the only way she dared resist was through tears and entreaties....

By this point I was really surprised. I have already told you that she had a stomach and two thighs that could envelope an average-sized man and that her arms could squeeze that same man to death. I interrupted her again and asked, "As big and fat as you are, why did you so easily let them beat you? Are you joking or telling the truth?"

She hesitated a moment and then burst out laughing. "I've only been fat for the last four years. At that time I was skinny and weak, so it was easy to bully me. You see, if you do this job forever, you've got to get fat."

That sounded absurd, but it really was like that. Doing that job every night destroys your health, maybe ten times more than normal, but getting fat makes you look as if you've been fortifying yourself with top-shelf ginseng and budding antler! Perhaps the expression "Heaven bears you, heaven maintains you" really is true for the brothel women.

She concluded, "Countless numbers of girls from respectable homes, and sometimes girls from high-born families, have had to get papers, and be tormented like that."

I asked her, "And what about you, how many girls have been tormented like that by your own hand?"

She stopped working the opium needle to emphasize the significance of her explanation for what she did. "That was a long time ago! There were maybe five or six girls.... In the past I was ready to be cruel, to get revenge for what life had done to me, but later on I started to think that in our place all of us were ill-fated, that everyone was miserable like me, so what fucking good did it do to be cruel to them? As the saying goes, 'Chickens of the same mother shouldn't hurt each other'; isn't that so? And, just recently, the government divided the sleeping room with iron bars to completely separate the girls with papers from the clandestine prostitutes, so girls cannot be cruel to others anymore!"

"Now, I have heard the rumor that girls who are good looking, young, and have papers get a lot of preferential treatment from their bosses."

"Definitely! Especially the girls who look aristocratic, high born. In Hanoi there are a few places with girls like that. When they go out on the street, all of the men think that they are high-class women because in the past they were high-class women. They never eat on the street side like the rest of us (because we don't really give a shit about keeping up appearances!).

Wherever they go, they go by car or rickshaw, but it's very rare that men can catch them going in and out of those red-numbered houses! When you see those girls on the street, at a festival, or in a market, the men all think that they are only female students! So how many playboys have taken on a lover who has previously held papers but mistakenly think that their cocks are getting a high-born maiden!"

◆◆◆

Yến had "held papers" for less than six months. She was among that group of women who made Dr. Coppin comment, "There are some who still look to be in the bloom of youth: they are the debutantes, who will soon wither."

Although according to the law Yến is an official courtesan, among the playboy set she is "an occasional," "a nice catch," or even a "girl from a respectable home." She does not have to receive soldiers, be they Asian, white, or black. Carpenters or blacksmiths who go to a brothel with only three hào in their pockets will never in anyone's lifetime get the pleasure of seeing her face in the waiting room, where courtesans like Lành sit like merchandise that a shop has on sale for cheap.

I asked her, "So you're not afraid that 'holding papers' will ruin you for the rest of your life?"

"What does that matter? It's actually the opposite. I can still make money like before, but I don't have the hassles with the Girls' Squad. I'm still hoping for a chance to become the lover of a Frenchman. I'd really like to have the position of those other women in the trade who have been more fortunate than me. It is only Vietnamese men who look down on having papers. The French think that the only really sure way is to go with girls who have papers."

I asked her further, "So how was it when you got papers?"

Yến responded simply, "I went with the Girls' Squad over to the Sûreté office to get my i.d., have my picture taken, get measured...."

"No, what did you think of it?"

Instead of responding, Yến asked me, "What did I think?"

"Yeah. Did you have any impressions about it? You didn't know that in doing so you had been placed in a category of people who don't live the same life as others? You weren't sorry about anything? You weren't worried about or scared of anything? You didn't know that once you've held papers, then that's it, that it's hard to marry a proper husband, because you've heard people say that 'tearing up papers' is very difficult for brothel girls?"

At this point Lành interjected, "It's my fault that that girl has papers, and bringing her back to my madam's place was my doing as well. She had only been put into the Dispensary one time, which meant that she was still free, but once she had left, what could she do to make a living other than get papers immediately?"

"So what about the girls who haven't reached the point where they have to get papers and are let out of the Dispensary; what usually happens to them?"

"The government officially advises them that they have to quit, that they can't work clandestinely forever, and the next time they are caught, they will be forced to get papers. In the past people were more decent. If a girl wanted to return to her village, the government would have someone transport her back to her village. But now, usually, mothers and fathers in the countryside only rarely want to take back such a nasty creature! No one wanted to cover the cost, so later on the regulations were dropped for transporting debauched country girls back to their native villages and turning them over to their parents."

I wanted to know the impressions of women when they first became official disciples of the Bạch My spirit....I couldn't know: they didn't have any impressions, so how could I know?

I couldn't know; for a long time now, they had no longer been "women." For a long time, although they did not have papers, they had already had the soul of a brothel girl. For them, holding papers was only another minor accident.

That evening I realized that I had wasted both my time and my money.

Lành was then down to the last dregs of the opium, and Yến, though she only "smoked for fun," had already taken her sixth pipe. Opium makes a person itchy, so Yến grimaced and squirmed about, scratching constantly.

I remembered that before entering this filthy room, I had bought a newspaper. I immediately sat up and walked over to the clothing rack to get the paper from my coat pocket. I went back toward the opium tray. I then found, mixed in with important news about the world, about the government, ten lines of trivial news:

Demi-Mondaine Arrested

Last night an officer of the Girls' Squad arrested Miss Ng. T. V., a *demi-mondaine* who has "had papers" for the past five years, in front of the door of the seedy hotel D. L. at approximately 4:00 a.m. A very large number of clients attempted to intervene on her behalf. The member of the Girls' Squad was determined to arrest her, but Ms. V. was determined to resist, yelling out that she had been living in the hotel for the past few days with her husband.

She held up and showed off a wad of money worth more than three hundred piasters, explaining that she was an upstanding person. However, Ms. V. was still sent to the Dispensary because she had yet to tear up her papers, even though she perhaps had been earning an honest living for the past five years. The authorities continue to investigate the matter.

I read this news aloud for Lành and Yến to hear. I waited for a reaction to appear on their faces.

Yến nodded in agreement and said to Lành, "Is that right? The old woman who gives us rice said that there was some such story in the *dít-băng-xe* just this morning."[5]

Lành calmly commented to me, "That's true all right. If you evade, you're gonna get arrested, even if you've evaded for ten years or five years. Who says not to tear up your papers! Getting arrested was the right thing, so what's there to complain and get upset about!"

I couldn't stop thinking about that trivial story....I remembered the story of the escaped criminal Jean Valjean, who had already attained the post of communal president, but the law came again to ask him about his earlier escape.[6] I was completely surprised that after hearing such a story, the two courtesans lying next to me were not in the least bit unsettled. But then I immediately understood it all. In this life, regardless of one's station, the immutable law of nature is this: no one wants to help anyone else get ahead!

Given that, I needed only to fully understand the reasons why it was difficult for a courtesan to tear up her papers, to change her ways, to turn a new leaf, in order to "start her life over again." Therefore, one more time I had to go look for Dr. Joyeux, the director of the Dispensary.

12

Tearing Up Papers

On that day more than ten men and women, whose tattered and untidy clothing showed that they belonged to Hanoi's poor (streetside water sellers, the unemployed, unsuccessful beggars, etc.), had come to seek the aid of the municipal physician, Dr. Nguyễn Huy Qùynh, an assistant to Dr. Joyeux. They had come to get medicine for infected eyes, sores, scabies, etc. Among them one could see a young, seriously dressed teenage boy sitting on the long bench. In his hand he held a set of rolled-up papers. He had the look of someone going to ask for something, with a face that showed deep worry.

When Dr. Qùynh opened the office door and stepped out to see the victims of inadequate hygiene who had come to the city for help, he looked first at the young man. That's the way life works. The person with respectable clothing, regardless of when or where, gets first consideration. Seeing that he was getting called, the young man stood up immediately and awkwardly said, "Sir, we would like to see the director of the Dispensary."

"What for? To ask for work or to ask for treatment?"

"Sir…we have a private matter."

"I am here to receive people in place of the director."

The young man dithered for a long time and then turned over the papers. After looking at the set of six sheets, Dr. Qùynh asked several of the nurses who worked for him to go examine the raggedly dressed patients. He then allowed the young man to enter the room and carefully closed the door.

Contained within that set of papers was not a request but a complaint. The young man wanted to bring a lawsuit against the Dispensary. A member of the Girls' Squad had arrested a young teenage girl, but the boy holding the petition held that she had been unjustly arrested. It was a serious matter!

In what follows below, we can get a rough sense of the heartfelt tale inscribed in that six-page petition.

◆◆◆

In an alley in the area around the cathedral, there is a middle-class family that, in a time of what had become all-consuming economic difficulties, decided to rent out some rooms to make some money. They had eight or nine lodgers—big young men, students of a private school, who were more serious about playing sports and chasing girls than they were about their studies. The young man with the above-mentioned letter of complaint was one of the students staying at that house.

Love had led the youngster into this messy business. But he who says "love" is also saying "lust" because the landlord of the house had a young girl who was excessively "romantic" and had promised herself to that young man.

In the beginning, they had innocently loved each other like in those splendid novels that speak of pure and noble love. But can that ever last! After they had come to trust each other and made up their minds to marry, they unexpectedly became…impatient.[1] The daily contact, combined with an unsatisfied hidden love, only served the interests of a malevolent force that was fanning a flame that both of them wanted to extinguish. On one side was the landlord's daughter, on the other the lodger; how could the parents know to intervene in time to protect against it? Faced with such longing, the young couple decided to go off and spend a night in a seedy hotel.

At five o'clock on the following morning, after the two of them had left the hotel and gone only a few dozen meters, an officer of the Girls' Squad, who had been lying in wait by the trunk of a tree for who knows how long, dashed over to them and asked the young girl to follow him to a place he thoughtfully and vaguely referred to as the "office." The lover, after vehemently protesting, was given the following response: "This has nothing to do with you, Sir. This woman works as a clandestine prostitute! I work for the government; I have a duty to arrest these types of people! You should know, Sir, that you are man number four!"

"I object! I guarantee that you are abusing your authority, acting illegally! We are not uneducated people, people who can't bite a grain of rice and crush it, whom you can bully! If you don't listen, we will file a suit with your superiors and then see! You must release this woman immediately! Not only has this woman never worked as a clandestine prostitute, but she is also going to be my wife!"

The Girls' Squad officer pursed his lips and calmly responded, "Sir, if you would like to file a suit against me, then file a suit! If, Sir, you bite into a grain of rice, then go ahead and crush it! Listen, Sir, I will be honest with you so you know: I only dare to make an arrest when I have enough evidence! My superiors would in no way tolerate the arrest of honest people! Anyway, Sir, today or tomorrow you will go and file your suit, but right now, I have to take this woman to the Dispensary!"

The girl looked down and cried, her hand weakly straining to break loose from the Girls' Squad officer's tight grip. Two or three rickshaw drivers had already pulled up around the three of them. The Girls' Squad officer pulled the girl up into one of them with him. His bicycle "sat" by itself in another rubber-wheeled rickshaw. The two rickshaws sped off, leaving the boy standing, shamed and stunned, between two nighttime rickshaw drivers.

One of the rickshaw drivers quickly jumped in, "If you want to file a suit, then take it to the Sûreté offices; I can take you there right now."

The other rickshaw driver, unconcerned about getting a fare, cut in: "You need to find the director of the Dispensary! I know about this stuff...."

The young man asked, "Is the director of the Dispensary at the Dispensary?"

"No! He's at the mayor's office, on the floor above the personal tax office. I know all about him! He sometimes rides around the entire night, looking around the side streets and alleyways to check on the work of the Girls' Squad."

Having learned that, the young man returned to the seedy hotel. How pitiful! It turned out that calamity had come violently and completely unexpectedly, such that the lad was panic stricken and no longer trusted his lover. He called the hotel boy, paid him, and then asked, "So! That 'scene' just now, that was a person who has occasionally worked as a prostitute for a long time?"

The hotel boy, like the majority of clever hotel boys who understand self-respect, immediately shook his head. "I don't know."

"That woman who came in, how many times has she been here?"

"Who can remember a face? Probably just one time."

"You're lying! If only one time, then why was she arrested?"

"Well, if she had gone into another seedy hotel a few times, who would ever know? I think she is an honest person or a prostitute; well, you—you slept with her, so surely you must understand...."

So at dawn that day, an uneducated hotel boy taught a useful lesson to a young student who was about to take the exam for his primary school diploma.[2] Oh! It turns out that people shouldn't close their eyes and believe women!

Although he was despondent and aggrieved because he was beginning to doubt the "love of his life," the young man didn't resign himself to throwing up his hands because in the heart of a man worthy of being called a man, whenever love has gone, compassion rushes in. Not everyone can cut off a love with one stroke. Moreover, when they went to the hotel, his "dear" had lied to her parents and said she was going back to their natal village so that she could go to the hotel, and the next morning she actually was going to go back to their village. So if she was being held in the Dispensary, it was an unmitigated disaster.

After encountering such misfortune, the lover didn't go back to his room the following morning. He went to an opium den to find a place to lie down and ponder how to write the petition. By 3 p.m. he had arrived at the mayor's office.

◆◆◆

Although he had already held his position for a long time, Dr. Nguyễn Huy Quỳnh was still easily moved and had yet to allow himself to be transformed by the work associated with his post, so he did not have the calm one often sees in officials who suffer from a "disease" that the French call a "professional deformation."

The student-like appearance of the person submitting the petition, his presentation of the case with anguish in his voice, the convincing explanation of the circumstances in which the woman could have been unjustly arrested had all made Dr. Nguyễn Huy Quỳnh very concerned. Moreover, he didn't dare to completely believe in the integrity of the Girls' Squad, like his own "superiors" did, so Dr. Quỳnh promised the unlucky lover that he would explain everything to Dr. Joyeux.

"But that's it for now. Dr. Joyeux is busy today with a council meeting at the mayor's office, so come here tomorrow at 9:00 a.m.; I will help put in a few words and see what the director decides."

"Sir, do you mean that the woman I am to marry must stay in the Dispensary tonight?"

"That is unavoidable! But don't worry; if she is examined and is disease-free, she will be released without question, unless this is her second arrest; then there's no need to mention...."

"Sir,...suppose that this is the second time, then what?"

"She'll have to get papers...."

"!"

"Unless there is someone who steps forward to tear up her papers for her, which is another story...."

The young man thanked him and then bid farewell while bowing before him with his hands clasped together.

In the afternoon, Dr. Nguyễn Huy Quỳnh, when presenting the letter of complaint to Dr. Joyeux, conscientiously explained all of the reasons for it:

the young woman who was arrested was from a respectable family, her father worked, the family rented rooms to almost ten students, so the Girls' Squad officer, basing his decision on Article 187 of the Police Law, perhaps mistakenly arrested an honest person.

Dr. Joyeux stopped his assistant.

"You shouldn't be excessively sympathetic or believe too much.... If you were a judge, then there wouldn't be a single thief who wasn't a victim of an injustice because the thief who is good at his trade also knows how to grovel, to weep, and to decry his injustice. The woman who was arrested here is very suspicious because a woman who is completely upstanding would never in her life go into a seedy hotel...."

"But the person with the petition has already declared to me that he will marry her...."

"I think that a woman who knows how to respect herself and is completely upstanding would never in her life go sleep in a seedy hotel, even if she was going with her real husband! Nevertheless, we already have that complaint, and we should be ready to carefully investigate it, so let me ask the Police des Moeurs and see what they say...."

The doctor then grabbed the telephone. Half an hour later he had a set of police reports on his desk. It turned out that in the previous eleven months or so the young woman who had been arrested had gone into four different seedy hotels with four different young men. The reports listed which seedy hotels she had entered, in which alleys, which streets, which days, what times; also which detective had seen her, which boy had given evidence—all of these things were laid out very clearly. The hotel boys keep an eye out for extremely foolish upstanding girls so they can potentially draw these sexually aroused girls into debauched circles. They were not at all reluctant to help out the Girls' Squad as unpaid apprentice detectives!

A member of the Girls' Squad therefore brought the reports to the director of the Dispensary and firmly asked Dr. Quỳnh to explain. "Sir, if there is a suit alleging an illegal arrest, I would like to be allowed to immediately call in the hotel boys who witnessed those events in order to give evidence before the person who filed the suit."

Dr. Joyeux groaned. "No, thank you; it's all right."

◆◆◆

The young student was granted a formal interview with Dr. Joyeux the following day.

"It would be best if you withdrew your petition. There are few times, once the Sûreté has done something, that someone has the grounds to sue it. I advise you to do that because I want you to avoid a large mess, because you could possibly be implicated in the lawsuit...."

Although he was deeply moved, the student remained eloquent on behalf of his love. "Sir, I do not believe the clandestine prostitution explanation because she is my wife."

"All right, where is your marriage certificate?"

"I'm sorry.... She is my fiancée...."

"Excuse me! If she truly is your fiancée, then that is something that the police will tolerate, but morality will not! No one goes off like that and sleeps in a seedy hotel with someone they have yet to marry! And a woman who will go with you into a filthy place like that has perhaps done the same thing with other men! If you are not that young woman's father or guardian, then you have no right to file this suit."

"Sir, I guarantee that that person is not a prostitute...."

"The police must not only suppress clandestine prostitution, but they must also protect against the spread of venereal diseases. Even if not engaged in prostitution, people can quite easily spread the venereal poison to others."

By this time the young man stood there numb, face bowed down, completely despondent.

The Dispensary director was moved and tried to console him.

"Don't worry about it. Your woman, if she has yet to contract a disease, will be released because it hasn't reached the point where she was arrested for working as a courtesan, when you would need to worry about asking to tear up her papers for her. And if she has a disease, then she will be held only until the disease has been cured, and then she will be released. You should be a bit more patient...."

"Sir, a young woman who has been arrested and put into the Dispensary has been humiliated enough already. Given that, is there any way to request her release immediately so that she is spared the 'duck's bill'?"

Dr. Joyeux confidently replied, "Certainly. If the young woman's father or guardian brings a letter here to request it and guarantees to the government that he will raise the young woman and keep her on the proper moral path. As for you, you are only the fiancé; you have no rights."

The young man stood there silently.... When a young woman from one of our upstanding families goes and sleeps in a seedy hotel, then is arrested and put into the Dispensary, does any father have the courage to bring himself to ask for anything in front of the authorities! Thus the ill-fated lover reluctantly withdrew the petition.

About five days later—long enough for a piece of glass to be taken over to the Municipal Hygiene office and a vile of blood to be taken to the Pasteur Institute so a "file" could be started to request the release of the "accused" young woman—the administrator in charge signed the papers that allowed her to leave the Dispensary.

But no one knows whether that furtive love led to marriage or to the parting of the young student and the daughter of the boarding house proprietor!

◆◆◆

The article in the government decision that lays out the procedures for brothel women to request the tearing up of their papers, which was signed by Resident Superior Rivet on February 3, 1921, is summarized only as follows:

> Article 8: All prostitutes, if they want to remove their name from the prostitution register, must prove that they have another reliable means of existence, or must demonstrate that there is an honorable, upstanding person who wants to support them, and that person must have sufficient means to care for her.
>
> The removal of the name will be decided by the responsible authorities, after they receive a statement from the police commissioner.[3]

The "responsible authority" here is either the mayor of Hanoi or the director of the Municipal Hygiene Office, who is concurrently the director of the Dispensary.

I don't know an Annamese person who knows how to respond when asked by a police officer about the conditions that must be met to tear up a courtesan's papers.... But I clearly do know that the phrase "adequate means to care for" has many different meanings.

Before all else that man must marry the courtesan and make her his wife, which means that he must first obtain a marriage certificate from the mayor's office. If he wants to get that marriage certificate, he must have a steady livelihood. If he is a trader, he must present his license. If he is a civil servant or works in a private office, he must have papers certifying that (that's very easy). If he doesn't work, doesn't trade, then he must show that he has property, has capital, so that he will live a steady, upstanding life with his wife. If he is not yet economically independent but has wealthy parents, then he must have a document from his parents that certifies that....

Dear reader, at this point, certainly there is someone who wants to shout out, "If it's like that...who would dare to think about marrying a woman from a brothel!" That's true, but the government can't be too tolerant because in the *Larousse* dictionary there are several words: *gigolo, maquereau, souteneur.* ...[4] Marrying a brothel woman is a bit difficult, but it is still quite "honorable": a police officer serves as the "matchmaker," and the mayor serves as the "best man!" The only difference from regular life is that the matchmaker doesn't lie to the bride's or the groom's families, and the best man has no illusions about the groom. To propose marriage to a "daughter" of the Bạch My spirit is not as easy (if it is easy) as asking the daughter of a retired mandarin. The Bạch My spirit is at bottom profoundly conservative (please do not misunderstand) and has always maintained this policy: a man marries a prostitute for her to be his wife; no one takes a wife for her to be a prostitute.[5] From ancient times, from East to West, the authorities have all shared this same policy.

I couldn't, as mentioned above, see one of my countrymen going to request the *tearing up of the papers* of a brothel girl....But Dr. Joyeux let me witness with my own eyes the case of a French soldier who wanted to marry a native courtesan.

◆◆◆

The soldier was a member of the Ninth Army Regiment, Hanoi. He was still very young. His name was...well, let's call him Untel for the time-being.[6] The girl whose papers the lad had asked to have torn up, Trần Thị Thiên Kim (there is no law that prevents prostitutes from giving themselves wonderful names like that), was also still young, had held papers for less than a year, and was a flower of the brothel world.[7] Their love had begun in a muddy pool, naturally. Perhaps Untel thought that Thiên Kim, though raised in the mud, was a lotus blossom. Love...one knows once its voice has been heard.

Untel, like a hundred thousand other magnanimous men, was never not going to be jealous once he was in love. To be jealous of a woman who works a job in which she is "there for the taking by all" is really absurd, but here we cannot talk about what is fair with Untel! People spread the rumor that every night, from 9:00 to 11:00 p.m., Untel left the base to go to the brothel, to sit there in one place, to silently stare at the other guests (yellow-skinned, white-skinned, black-skinned), to haunt the madam, to grumble at his lover, to hinder "business." Once the madly-in-love lad started a fight with some other white soldiers. Unable to take it any longer, one day the proprietress shook her finger at Untel and said in accented French, "Get out of here! You don't have the right to sit here and bother the other guests! You really love her, huh? If you do, why don't you just have done with it and marry her!"[8]

Thiên Kim added, "*Ami,* marry me!"

Ah, it turns out that it was as simple as that, but the lad had thought about it forever and couldn't figure it out. That was it; he'd just be done with it; he no longer needed to fear that constant jealousy would shorten his life. The next day, Untel went to the police station with a written request....

If he had been like other people, happy to be getting married, happy to be carrying out the procedures to marry immediately, then the officer wouldn't have had to worry about any complications. It would have been simply a matter of doing the paperwork and sending it up to the mayor for a signature, and then the two would be a "happily wedded couple." But Untel's character was out of the ordinary. The jealousy in his blood had made him suspicious. He was asking to tear up the papers for Thiên Kim so that they could live together as husband and wife, like one hundred thousand soldiers with one hundred thousand other native women, that was all; but the marriage formalities at the mayor's office were important, and he couldn't make a decision right there on the spot! Not knowing what to do, the officer in charge of this matter invited Untel to go speak with Dr. Joyeux.

As he had already received the paperwork from the police office, Dr. Joyeux sent an orderly out when he was given Untel's calling card.

"The director is busy with work this morning, so he is not receiving guests."

In the afternoon Untel came again. He informed the orderly, "I am a soldier, and getting permission to take time off is very difficult; tell the director that he should try to set aside some time to receive me. Thank you."

But the messenger had already been warned.... Even though Dr. Joyeux was sitting on the other side of the door, the messenger said, "But he's not in the office! Today he is busy teaching at the university. Please come back again tomorrow afternoon." After grumbling ineffectually, Untel again resigned himself to going home.

When he told me this story, Dr. Joyeux explained, "I had to create annoying complications for them in order to get a discreet look at their psychological state. If they sincerely loved each other, then no matter how many annoyances there were, they would still resolve to return. But if they did not come back, then that was fortunate for them too, because if they quickly became discouraged by a small matter, then they certainly wouldn't persist with the big things, especially when marriage is a mixing of two opposite characters who must both contain themselves. The majority of soldiers who marry prostitutes do it because they are drunk, because they are in a momentary state of elation.... Therefore, getting married is easy; getting divorced is also easy, and after only a little while we again see that the woman who has made the turn must again turn back toward the road of prostitution."

Four days later, Untel was at last able to get permission for a leave and arrived at the mayor's office. When he saw that very young face, Dr. Joyeux was immediately scared of the lad's impulsiveness.... But Untel seemed to have checked Rivet's decision.

Dr. Joyeux started, "Sir, we cannot immediately erase that girl's name."

"Sir, are the native women trustworthy enough that the government forces the people who ask to tear up their papers to marry them immediately? We first need to understand each other; we need to live with each other for awhile.... Sir, please lower the requirements here because lowering the requirements is something that probably can be done."

Dr. Joyeux then began to negotiate.

"Or let us lower the requirements like this: although we won't have completely erased her name, that woman will receive three months of temporary freedom; she need not go to the Dispensary, stay in the brothel, or obey the laws regulating prostitution.... If after three months...of probation—excuse me, if we can call it that—it seems that you two can marry, then you can get the marriage certificate issued, and I will issue an order erasing her name completely."

"We are asking to tear up her papers completely."

Dr. Joyeux responded, "The government cannot give you satisfaction on that."

Untel then stood up, changing into the voice of the law. "Sir, I have the right to ask for the tearing up of her papers, and it must be done because Article 8 of the decision of February 3, 1921, states that a prostitute can ask to tear up her papers when she has an honorable person who is in need of her and when that honorable person has adequate means for taking care of her; that's all. The decision does not compel the person making the request to take the prostitute as a wife, so we want to know for what reasons you are forcing me to register the marriage!"

Dr. Joyeux gave a slight, scornful smile. "Excuse me! You know that law, and we know it very well too. But you are forgetting one thing: you are forgetting that you are a soldier! You also don't understand the clause that states, 'The person requesting the removal of a woman's name is only required to have sufficient means to care for her'; it is written as such because the government wants to be accommodating to either the parents or a sponsor, so that they can ask on behalf of a daughter or someone under their protection, so that that prostitute can start her life over again and escape from depraved circles.…For one thing, you are neither the parent nor the sponsor of this woman named Kim Thiên, but you also don't definitively want to marry her, so you have no right to ask to remove her name from the prostitution register! We can guarantee to you that that's how it is."

Untel stood there stunned, like a person who had died standing. Sweat soaked his forehead. At last the lad had to apologize to Dr. Joyeux and asked to be excused to go and "think about it carefully." After that he would come back…for further instruction. The jealousy, which before had warned him to be suspicious, later made him decide. Two weeks later he registered the marriage with Thiên Kim before the court.

Dr. Joyeux apologetically explained to me, "A French soldier marrying a native prostitute in accordance with the law—I know that has no benefit for France, but it does eliminate one source of harm caused by venereal disease and improves the lot of one soldier in the army of prostitutes. If it is too easy for them, then in only a few months the man will abandon his wife, and the woman will return to debauchery, if she hasn't been forced by her husband to go back to prostitution to take care of her gigolo."

◆◆◆

After taking leave of Dr. Joyeux, I went to see his deputy, Mr. Nguyễn Huy Quỳnh. I raised the issue of the woman who had fled from the Dispensary five years before and had been arrested again, at a time when she had over 300 piasters. This incident had positively demonstrated the integrity of that Girls' Squad officer because when you've got 300 piasters in your hands, you can buy the conscience of many people! Mr. Nguyễn Huy Quỳnh told me, "Arresting girls who have a very large amount of money on them is very common. On those occasions, Inspector Mas, in front of the Dispensary employees and the girl who was arrested, will carefully confirm its value a great many times because he is very afraid of being discredited; he's very cautious."

"Sir, what happened to that woman?"

"She had to hold papers again."

"She had to hold papers again when she had more than 300 piasters in her hand?" I was stunned.

"Certainly! How do we know that that's not money earned in clandestine prostitution! Do you think that once they have money, they can give up the habit of playing around, of chasing after money?"

"Then what if that woman really had a husband?"

"If her statements were true, then certainly her husband would come and get her."

"Otherwise?"

"Otherwise she would have to stay in a brothel again or hold private papers; they are free to decide!"

"So if it's like that, once you've held papers, it's unlikely that you'll escape from this pool of tears?"

"If you don't have your parents or relatives come and get you."

I had already grieved for the Kiềus of that time. In order to stop myself from crying questionable tears, I had to think about the lines "bad karma from the sins of a past life" and then "karmic retribution."

WHAT DOES THE FUTURE HOLD?

On March 20, 1928, the League of Human Rights in France, of which Mr. Basch served as president, convened at the headquarters of the Literature Association in Paris in order to condemn the past and present laws regulating the brothel trade.[9] More than one thousand people were in attendance. Everyone agreed that the laws restricting prostitution ran counter to the guiding principle of the equality of all before the law, be they male or female; that arrests by the Police des Moeurs were often arbitrarily conducted; and that more than a few of the arrests were damaging to official prostitutes and often damaging to women from upstanding families too.... The purpose of the session was to obtain the unanimous approval of a petition that requested the following:

> It is considered: The regulation of prostitution is unjust, because its laws place one group of people outside of the law; the preservation of public health exists only in name because men are not examined; it is autocratic because only a very small number of women in the trade are examined; it is also dangerous because once the people trust the government that the female prostitutes are definitely healthy, it is much easier for them to contract a disease.... We therefore request that the authorities change the present savage law and place it under the common law regime and use all legal methods to eliminate prostitution in all cities.[10]

That was the day that a reform movement shook the prejudices of the conservative faction, which wanted to eliminate prostitution through severe measures; among this faction was Senator Bérenger.

In early February 1937, about ten years later, an international conference was held to discuss the elimination of prostitution and the sale of humans in the Far East. The meeting was held in Bandung (in the Dutch East Indies), and the French government finally stated that it was ready to reform the legal regime for prostitution that was currently in force in the mother country and all of the colonies. The French government's representative at that session was Mr. Labrouquère, a professor from the Hanoi law school.[11]

In a detailed presentation, the professor sought to clearly explain to other nations the past and present policies that France had used to deal with prostitution in Africa and in the Far Eastern colonies. After reminding the other nations of the stance of the French representatives a few years before in Geneva, when they had argued that the regulation of prostitution was a domestic political matter, Professor Labrouquère then noted that France shared the opinion of other countries that have asserted that from an international perspective, common law must be the pillar for "abolitionism." But as for abolishing the old regime in the colonies, the professor was very cautious with his words:

> The enactment of an abolitionist regime in Indochina will founder due to many major obstacles because in Indochina records regarding curriculum vitae, births, deaths, and marriages are still unclear; primary education has yet to become widespread; public health efforts have problems; and ultimately the people are still extremely ignorant. As a result, the methods used to eliminate venereal diseases must be appropriately adjusted to fit with the level of the people. Professor Labrouquère again explained about the preparations of the medical service in Indochina to definitively get rid of all brothels and open many more hospitals in order to easily provide patients with medication. In Indochina it is hoped that if the living standards and educational levels of the people increase, then the prostitution problem will also diminish. One point could be believed with certainty: once the Parliament had approved Sellier's draft law, it would then be implemented in all of the colonies, and it would unify all of the methods used to eliminate prostitution and put them in accordance with international public opinion. ARIP, February 1937.[12]

We understand from this information that the French government will soon have a new policy: the Sellier draft law. Mr. Sellier is actually the minister of public health who drafted the law in an abolitionist spirit (abolish the old regime and replace it with a new regime), so that society could avoid the unjust and inhumane aspects associated with the elimination of prostitution and venereal diseases.

On this point, we should note that compared to all other countries in the world, France is the most conservative and lags the farthest behind. In 1928, the League of Nations approved a resolution authorizing the closure of all brothels. The French League for the Restoration of Public Morality (Ligue Française pour le Relèvement de la Moralité Publique) has declared that in the nineteenth century nearly all the now civilized, progressive countries of Europe and America had to borrow laws regulating prostitution from France. They took those laws and discarded them long ago.[13]

So, what is abolitionism?[14]

Founded upon the equality of men and women, abolitionism has the strong and vocal support of women's liberation groups.... Women cannot forever remain the "sex slaves" of a prostitution trade that the government recognizes and protects; women cannot forever be required to exclusively submit to being pursued, examined, and then incarcerated when they have a disease! In fact, these opinions are very fair and humane, and if one seeks the realization of these aspirations, the abolitionist policy includes several activities that will eliminate impediments to the freedom of women, such as closing all brothels or any places that lead to debauchery; eliminating the group of people who live off of the "flower and moon" trade (seedy hotel owners, madams, pimps, boys who arrange for girls, etc.); hunting down those engaged in the international trade in humans, while also nurturing industries that use the labor of women and girls, etc.... The government must above all else set a shining example by withdrawing the restrictive laws. There will be no more "prostitutes with papers" and no more public institutions exclusively reserved for prostitutes. The Police des Moeurs, as a result, will lose its reason to exist because the punishments for prostitution-related crimes will be dealt with in court and the police will only carry out arrests. As for venereal disease, it can be combatted through sex education in schools; films, forums, leaflets, posters; providing the public with very easy methods to treat venereal diseases; the trial and severe punishment of people, male or female, who transmit venereal diseases to others; the requirement that diseases be treated until they are completely cured; the issuance of a certificate by a doctor prior to marriage or before a woman goes to work as a wet nurse, etc. Listening to this, one knows well enough that "abolitionism" is a splendid ideal, but implementing it is no easy matter. Doctor Joyeux has already said so:

With respect to those people who want to speak of this only in order to deceive others, this is a very modest method for solving the prostitution problem in a country because in implementing this policy, a country need not attain a very high level of evolution or organization, but the countries that follow this policy today have yet to reach a point in which it is done appropriately or adequately; implementing that ideal means guaranteeing that your country does not have poverty and hunger; that population registers are carefully kept even though their numbers go up and down daily; that government registers and papers are carefully maintained on even trivial matters; that an adequate intellectual standard is widespread and the people understand their civil rights and know the law in a way they can be proud of; that the medical service has an adequate number of hospitals, employees, and medicines, to the point of having a surplus; to summarize, it is a declaration that your country is already wealthy and strong, is already extremely civilized. I think that Indochina has yet to reach that level.

If you want to do it skillfully, to really get good results, you must follow a more modest policy. You must make adjustments because the vast majority of the women in this country are extremely different from each other, depending upon each particular area and the specific climatic, political, administrative, and societal situations; there are only a few intellectuals who are completely Westernized, and there are still some tribes that remain as barbarous as people in ancient times. The countryside produces an untold number of women who work as prostitutes, and they are still uneducated. If some women in the cities are civilized and progressive, in contrast, 99 percent of the other women are still inferior in every way when compared to men. Even in Hanoi, many times people forget to register a birth. Apart from their daily tasks, which are difficult and require little thought, women here are often so ignorant that they are unaware of the events taking place around them. This general impoverishment creates the conditions for the loosening of morals and ethics, combined with an ethic that disregards male-female sexual relations and a careless and unreflective spirit.

Furthermore, the organization of the administration, the justice system, the police, and hygiene here are still inadequate. State funds do not allow for large amounts of money to be spent on necessary projects. Because of these challenges, a clever policy that fits with the times is to adjust the old legal regulations through a humane pardoning of the group of women who are currently evolving, to prepare them so that they will have the capacity to benefit from Sellier's draft law, which the Parliament will approve.

In this country, people cannot completely line up behind the *regulationist* faction, just as they cannot completely line up behind the *abolitionist* faction, but they must approach things *according to the circumstances,* which means *evolution.* The essential point is that we should not line up behind the *"do nothing"* faction—which would mean never budging in the face of this catastrophe, as we lazily rely upon the excuse that there is no theory that will lead to completely satisfactory results—because we have already seen a great deal of damage associated with prostitution.

Those reasons are very easy to understand. This country has yet to reach a level in which it can genuinely benefit from Sellier's draft law. As Dr. Joyeux is the secretary of the Prophylactic League (Ligue Prophylactique) and the Committee for the Elimination of Venereal Diseases, which was established by the governor general, when he speaks it is as if an official of the governor general were speaking. The policy for dealing with prostitution has been and will be: *according to the circumstances.*

At present the governor general's office is conducting research on laws for suppressing those people who survive on the "moon and flower, bees and butterflies" trade. It is also researching plans to build more hospitals, establish schools to train male and female nurses for a new service in which they will go to individual houses to teach about venereal diseases *(social visits),* and set up a sanitary police service so that perhaps one day in the future there can be a genuine promulgation of abolitionism *(integral abolitionism)* for the women of Indochina. Such plans will actually implement the program of Dr. Le Roy des Barres.

Until that day, there will be many changes in Vietnamese society, many "revolutions," many "troubles." The government will get rid of the Dispensary, disband the Girls' Squad, close the seedy hotels. The courts will throw the streetwalkers, the pimps, and the people who spread venereal diseases into jail. In the primary schools, they will teach young people the things they need to know about sexual relations when they are still in puberty!

Get rid of the Dispensary because it can hold only some two hundred women when there are five or six thousand other clandestine prostitutes freely spreading venereal diseases among the people.

Close the brothels because in Clemenceau's opinion, it is not only the women who hold papers or work clandestinely that participate in prostitution, so there's no compelling reason for placing those women outside of society!

Abolish the Girls' Squad because that service is an embarrassment to civilized nations—many strong nations today have already gotten rid of theirs—and because that service will have no work to do if the city closes the Dispensary. Also, imprison those men who have a disease but still seek out sexual pleasures because that is an offense that should be punished without mercy.

Instruct the youth about the problems of sexual relations because the self-conscious spirit of the "misguided" moralists has already led to many damaging consequences; because if you don't teach the young, then they naturally "know"; and when they don't clearly know, they will catch diseases or weaken their mental faculties because they masturbate.

To summarize in one sentence: Sellier's draft law will repair many injustices in our society; there is no reason to resign ourselves to looking at the plight of only the tens of thousands of women who engage in prostitution because they want to escape starvation and then are hunted down, maltreated, thrown into jail, forced to *hold papers,* or have difficulty marrying a respectable husband, while at the same there are countless others engaged in clandestine prostitution but who are mandarins who rule over their husbands, travel by car, live in multistoried homes, have power, influence, and honor, and are regarded as important women, princesses, ladies!

But if we want to reach that stage, I ask those who think about society, who love life, whose blood has reached a temperature that makes them indignant about these injustices, to become a bit more zealous. Journalists, people's representatives—if you truly want to liberate our country's women so they can escape from prostitution's enslaving regime—you should prepare to demand Sellier's law with the same zealousness that you demand Freedom. Because if no one budges at all, then the authorities will be in no hurry to do anything, and every time it must respond, the government will once again respond in the way that it always responds to us: "The Annamese people still lack the capacity."

But who knows when men who genuinely want to liberate women will appear? Or perhaps this society, which has been debased a thousand times, can have only men who are opportunists, who consider the improvement of society as the equivalent of flattering the base desires of women and girls. Whether it is dishonest or sincere, they are offenders against civilization, against morals; do they not know that instead of saving our weakened race from depravity, they push this pitiable group, first into "romanticism" and then into prostitution's muddy pool?

1937

HANOI STREET NAMES

Colonial Name	Contemporary Name
Án Sát Siêu	Ngõ Gạch
Boulevard Rollandes	Hai Bà Trưng
Chợ Hôm	Chợ Hôm
Cửa Đông	Cửa Đông
Đào Duy Từ	Đào Duy Từ
Đường Thành	Đường Thành
Gia Ngư	Gia Ngư
Hàng Bột	Tôn Đức Thắng
Hàng Buồm	Hàng Buồm
Hàng Cân	Hàng Cân
Hàng Lọng	Lê Duẩn
Hàng Mành	Hàng Mành
Hàng Thịt	Unknown
Hàng Trống	Hàng Trống
Julien Blanc	Phủ Doãn
Khâm Thiên	Khâm Thiên
Mã Mây	Mã Mây
Nam Ngư	Nam Ngư
Paul Bert Square	Vườn Indira Gandhi
Quán Thánh	Quán Thánh
Rue Balny	Trần Nguyên Hãn
Rue Rodier	Thi Sạch
Tràng Tiền	Tràng Tiền
Vạn Thái	Unknown
Yên Thái Alley	Ngõ Yên Thái

THE DISPENSARY'S INTERNAL REGIME

French doctors managing the Dispensary had a long-standing concern about the lack of discipline inside. Dr. Piquemal, who worked as the director of the Dispensary for several years in the mid-1920s, commented that "The patients under treatment in the Dispensary are a very particular group, essentially undisciplined" (RST 78701). Over the decades, various doctors and officials had attempted to routinize internal practices in order to make the Dispensary run more smoothly.

There is no existing document that definitively describes the Dispensary's internal regime, but several documents give a general picture. One of the first extant documents was the proposed daily schedule that Dr. Piquemal submitted to the mayor for transmission to the resident superior of Tonkin. A common refrain about the Dispensary was that it had a carceral character, and a review of the eighteen articles in Piquemal's schedule support this claim (RST 78701). In his scheme, a normal day went as follows:

6:00–6:45	Wake-up and clean-up of sleeping area.
6:45–7:00	Free time for purchasing food or supplementary items.
7:00–10:00	Medical care and work.
10:00–11:00	Rest and organization of the refectory.
11:00–14:00	Siesta and recreation.
14:00–17:00	Medical care and work.
17:00–17:45	Rest and organization of the refectory.
17:45	Recreation.
19:00	Bedtime.
20:00	Lights out.

Piquemal's proposal was the foundation for the decree passed on August 9, 1928, that clarified the Dispensary's internal functioning, though the decree did not include a timed schedule. As Phụng describes in the text, the decree was notable for forbidding alcohol, opium, and games of chance, and it also established the punishments for internal rule violations and evasions. Tellingly, it prohibited "conversations in a loud voice." Communication with people outside of the Dispensary also had to be authorized and required the presence of the chief supervisor or one of her assistants (see Joyeux 1930, 644).

NOTES

INTRODUCTION

1. The literature on the sociocultural dimensions and discourses on prostitution and venereal disease is, as Gail Hershatter has written, "far too complex to summarize here" (1999, 5), yet several works merit mention, with Hershatter's *Dangerous Pleasures: Prostitution and Modernity in Twentieth-Century Shanghai* (1999) prominent among them. For prostitution in other French colonies, the work of Christelle Taraud, notably her monograph *La prostitution coloniale: Algérie, Tunisie, Maroc (1830–1962)* (2003), provides a definitive examination. For the British colonies, Luise White's *The Comforts of Home: Prostitution in Colonial Nairobi* (1990) and Philippa Levine's *Prostitution, Race and Politics: Policing Venereal Disease in the British Empire* (2003) demonstrate with great insight the sociocultural complexities of prostitution and venereal disease in the British Empire. Mary Spongberg's *Feminizing Venereal Disease: The Body of the Prostitute in Nineteenth-Century Medical Discourse* (1997) provides a compelling account of the associations between female bodies and venereal disease in nineteenth-century Britain.

2. Zinoman 2002 provides the most comprehensive introduction to Phụng's life.

3. The English translation is available in Lockhart 1996.

4. English translations of *Kỹ Nghệ Lấy Tây* and *Cơm Thầy Cơm Cô* can be found in Vũ Trọng Phụng 2006 and Lockhart 1996 respectively.

5. The publication dates were January 21 and 28; February 2 and 18; March 4, 11, 18, and 25; and April 1, 8, and 15. The original newspaper title was *Lục-Sì: Phóng Sự Dài Về Nhà Phúc Đường Phố Hỏa Lò* (*Lục Xì:* A Long *Reportage* on the Charitable Establishment on Hỏa Lò Street).

6. In both published and archival materials, French doctors working in colonial Indochina frequently used only their last names, which were sometimes written only in capital letters without accents. All efforts have been made to present the doctors' names and spellings as accurately as possible.

7. The regulations regarding prostitution in Hanoi were revisited and revised on a number of occasions during the colonial period. The fullest account of them can be found in Joyeux 1930:614–645. The discussion that follows presents only their main, shared features. For a comprehensive discussion of regulation and the issues faced by French doctors and officials, both civilian and military, see Rodriguez 2001 and Guénel 2001.

8. A full accounting of the Dispensary's staffing in 1937 can be found in Ligue Prophylactique de la Ville de Hanoi 1937, 2–3.

9. In 1937, Vietnamese physicians in colonial Indochina were collectively known as "Indochinese doctors." A small number had earned the medical doctor degree and were referred to in Vietnamese as doctor, or *bác sĩ*. Others, such as Nguyễn Huy Quỳnh, whom Phụng encounters in the text, achieved the lower rank of "assistant physician" *(y sĩ)*.

10. The league had been set up in October 1934 under the leadership of Hanoi's mayor, Edouard Henri Virgitti, and Bernard Joyeux, the Dispensary director. Its history and functions are discussed in Ligue Prophylactique de la Ville de Hanoi 1937.

11. For example, in 1896 there were sixteen licensed brothels (MH 2580), in 1914 and 1915 there were twenty-eight (Coppin 1930, 568), in 1923 there were twenty-two (Le Roy des Barres 1924, 8), and in 1928 there were twenty (Le Roy des Barres 1929, 704). The primary reason for the sharp reduction in the number of licensed brothels after 1915 was the closure of the seven "Japanese houses" *(maisons japonaises)*, brothels that had existed in Hanoi from the early years (see MH 2580) and employed only Japanese prostitutes. These so-called *musumés* (the Japanese term for daughter) were renowned in French colonial circles for their "cleanliness," a reference to their apparently lower rates of venereal disease infection.

12. Complaints of abuse were not unique to the Vietnamese system, as officers in France also had abuse charges leveled against them.

13. See appendix 2 for complete details of the schedule.

14. Although other journalists received access to the Dispensary at the time of Phụng's first visit, only he and Thao Thao published accounts of their visits.

15. White (1990) provides a thought-provoking discussion of the multiple paths to prostitution in colonial Kenya.

16. Currency in colonial Hanoi was calculated as follows: 1 xu/sous was 1 cent, 10 xu equaled 1 hào, and 10 hào equaled one piaster.

17. Trachoma was another prominent cause of blindness.

CHAPTER 1. A BLEMISH ON THE CITY

1. Edouard Henri Virgitti served as Hanoi's mayor from December 1933 until November 1938. Born in 1886 in Algiers, Virgitti was a decorated World War I veteran who first arrived in Indochina in 1905. He served in various posts during an almost thirty-year career in the colonial administration and could speak Vietnamese. Although his tenure as mayor was marked by controversies over tax increases, he was very active in trying to improve public health in Hanoi. In late 1937, after Phụng's encounter with him, he orchestrated a successful campaign to prevent a severe cholera epidemic from ravaging the city. He left Hanoi in early November 1938 due to ill health (MH 1127).

2. The Sûreté Générale was the colonial administration's police service for pub-

lic security. Its responsibilities included the collection of intelligence on various per-ceived threats to the colonial regime, notably those posed by political dissidents and anticolonial organizations.

3. In the original text, Phụng included the following French quotation, "Tout acte de la vie sexuelle, même sur forme de prostitution, netant [*sic*] après tout que l'exercise du droit que chacun possède d'user ou d'abuser de sa personne." An identi-cal version of the quotation can be found in Abadie-Bayro 1930, 550.

4. Phụng invokes the Bạch My spirit, or White Browed Spirit, as a metonym for the entire prostitution industry, as it was the guardian spirit of prostitution. The relationship between a particular spirit and trade was common in Hanoi; all of the city's famous guilds, each ensconced on its own street in the "36 Guild Streets" (36 Phố Phường) area of the old quarter, had its own guardian spirit, for which guild members regularly conducted rites. Although it no longer exists, a photograph of the shrine to the Bạch My spirit within the Municipal Dispensary compound can be found in Thao Thao's *reportage* on the dispensary (Thao Thao, February 2, 1937, 1) and in Ligue Prophylactique de la Ville de Hanoi 1937. Reference to this spirit and rites for it performed by prostitutes are also made in *The Tale of Kiều,* lines 930–934.

5. The expression "a thousand-year civilization" *(nghìn năm văn vật)* is a poetic metaphor that refers to Hanoi. It derived from King Lý Thái Tổ's establish-ment of the city of Thăng Long, an earlier name for Hanoi, as his capital in the year 1010.

CHAPTER 2. THE MUSE OF THE DISPENSARY GIRLS

1. Bernard Joyeux was born in 1899 in Langres, France. After serving in the French military during the World War I, he began working as a physician for the city of Hanoi in 1926, when he was a member of the Indigenous Medical Assistance (Assistance Médicale Indigène). He was appointed as the first director of the Hygiene Service of the City of Hanoi, which Phụng simplifies as the Municipal Hygiene Ser-vice, on January 1, 1930, and remained in the post until January 1939. An active researcher on numerous topics with an impressive publication record, Joyeux was also on faculty at the Hanoi-based Medical School of Indochina (MH 870). Joyeux was thirty-seven at the time of his interview with Phụng.

2. Jim Gérald (1889–1958) was a popular French actor of the 1930s. Phụng's awareness of foreign movie stars is not surprising. Hanoi had several cinemas that showed foreign films, and many of Hanoi's major Vietnamese-language newspapers regularly had articles on cinema.

3. In the text, Phụng employed two terms for what are now referred to as "Viet-nam" and "the Vietnamese." Occasionally he used the contemporary terms "Viet-nam" and "the Vietnamese," but more frequently he used the forms common during

the colonial period, "Annam" and "Annamese." Despite the different terms, the references are to the same categories.

4. The text from this line up to "Because that boss is ordering" was not included in the Vũ Trọng Phụng 1999 version of *Lục Xì*, reportedly after having been lost. The text here is from the version in Phan Trọng Thưởng, Nguyễn Cừ, and Nguyễn Hữu Sơn 2000, 778–779.

5. The first three texts were all published by Joyeux in the *Bulletin de la Société Médico-Chirurgicale de l'Indochine*: Joyeux 1930, 1934a, and 1934b respectively. The last ("The Venereal Peril and Methods to Combat It") was also likely written by Joyeux, though it is unclear if it was published under that title.

6. Bảo Đại (1913–1997) was Vietnam's last emperor. He ascended the throne in 1932, abdicated in 1945, but returned to serve as head of state from 1949 to 1955.

7. Virgitti and Joyeux 1938.

8. After the dissemination of this song, all prostitutes held in the dispensary were required to memorize and be able to completely recite its words as a precondition for release. They were also required to correctly recite it if asked by a dispensary doctor (Ligue Prophylactique de la Ville de Hanoi 1937, 11).

9. The remaining lines of the poem are in Vũ Trọng Phụng 2000b, 781–782.

10. One significant stanza in "The Ballad of Eros" that appeared in the newspaper edition but was edited out of the book version read as follows:

> Hold the penis from below,
> From the base to the hole at its end.
> If you see even a little pus there, watch out!
> That's where the danger comes from;
> You must pay attention; don't play with it!
> Then look at his penis,
> See if there are any strange marks.

The beginning of this stanza describes how to identify a gonorrhea infection.

CHAPTER 3. A FEW STATISTICS AND A LITTLE HISTORY

1. Phụng quotes here from Article 11 of the decree of April 28, 1886, which dealt with prostitution in Tonkin. The complete text of the decree can be found in Joyeux 1930, 614–615. Phụng's historical discussion is informed by Ligue Prophylactique de la Ville de Hanoi 1937, 1–2, which also drew from Coppin 1930, 571.

2. Phụng alludes here to a common rural Vietnamese proverb, "Sell your distant relations, buy your close neighbors" *(Bán anh em xa, mua láng giềng gần).*

3. The adage Phụng employs here criticizes people who, once their basic needs are met, are more interested in seeking pleasure than attending to serious issues.

4. See Abadie-Bayro 1930, 540.

5. Phụng quotes here from a passage in Joyeux 1932, 333. Joyeux also commented, however, that Keller had informed him that at least 70 percent of blindness cases were caused by exposure to gonococcus.

6. Phụng's usage of "terms of avoidance" *(lối nói kiêng)* refers to the practice in colonial Vietnam of prohibiting direct comments on certain topics or conditions, such as the case of syphilis in children described in the text, and the use of euphemisms or other terms in their place.

7. The original text from which Phụng draws is found in Joyeux 1932, 335–336. However, he makes several minor modifications in his translation.

8. The Hôpital Indigène was the main facility in Hanoi for treating Vietnamese patients. Established in 1904, it was located near the Dispensary.

9. The original text from which Phụng draws is found in Joyeux 1930, 502–503. However, he makes several additions that are included here.

10. Dr. Adrien Le Roy des Barres was one of the longest-serving physicians in colonial Hanoi. He had worked as an intern in Paris before beginning his service in Hanoi in 1902. In addition to working as a professor in the School of Medicine of Indochina, he had held almost every senior medical position in Hanoi, including director of the Dispensary. He published voluminously on numerous topics and continued to publish until the early 1940s (MH 923).

CHAPTER 4. THERE MUST BE HARM

1. These comments and the one below were made by Dr. P. Bodros, a French physician who worked in Hanoi in the late 1920s. He was in fact a finalist for the position of director of the Municipal Hygiene Service that was given to Dr. Joyeux (MH 870). He later served as the director of the Municipal Hygiene Service in Haiphong. The text from which Phụng quotes is unknown, although Charbonnier (1936, 72) lists in his bibliography a text by Bodros entitled "Le Péril Vénérien et la Prostitution à Haïphong" (The Venereal Peril and Prostitution in Haiphong), but he did not record the date or place of publication.

2. *Refoulement* is a psychoanalytical concept developed by Sigmund Freud that involves the repression of powerful and dangerous desires in the unconscious. Phụng had an interest in Freudian ideas regarding human sexuality, a point evident in the life story of the character Huyền in *Làm Đĩ* (Peter Zinoman, personal communication).

3. The Patenôtre Treaty, named after the French diplomat Jules Patenôtre de Noyers, who negotiated it, definitively established the French protectorate over Tonkin and Annam.

4. Phủ Doãn hospital was another name for the Hôpital Indigène.

CHAPTER 5. STROLLING INSIDE THE DISPENSARY

1. Justin Godart (1871–1956) was a prominent French politician who had served as minister of health in 1932 and was active in international public health issues. He visited Indochina in February 1937 as part of an inspection mission organized by the Popular Front government to plan social reforms. The left-leaning Popular Front government championed reform in France and its colonies.

2. According to the Western calendar, the date was Tuesday, February 9, 1937.

3. Given the specifics of the lunar calendar in 1937, the Vietnamese Lunar New Year (Tết Nguyên Đán) was to begin on Thursday, February 11. The Lunar New Year celebrations, referred to simply as Tết, are the most important family holidays in Vietnam; thus the absence of journalists two days before is not surprising.

4. Félix Mas was born in Leynhac, France, in 1892 and joined the Hanoi police in 1915. His involvement with the Service des Moeurs began in 1929. He received a number of awards and extensive praise from his superiors for his conduct as a police officer (MH 945).

5. Phụng refers here to line 923 in The Tale of Kiều, when the heroine Kiều encounters for the first time Tú Bà, the madam of the brothel into which she has been sold.

6. The "mangoes" were a slang reference to the swelling of the lymph nodes in the groin caused by venereal lymphogranuloma.

7. The text to which Phụng refers is Le Dispensaire Antivénérien Municipal et la Ligue Prophylactique de la Ville de Hanoi. According to his comments in the text, Phụng did not actually receive the text from Dr. Joyeux in his earlier visit to his office, but as Joyeux was a leading member of the league, he was a likely source for it (see Ligue Prophylactique de la Ville de Hanoi 1937).

8. The Institute of Radium of Indochina (l'Institut du Radium de l'Indochine) was established in 1923 and was the premier research and treatment center for cancer in colonial Indochina.

9. Joyeux reported that the women were allowed to leave for forty-eight hours and all returned on time. He also commented that "A discreet investigation allowed us to confirm that none among them had consecrated herself to Venus" (Ligue Prophylactique de la Ville de Hanoi 1937, 16).

CHAPTER 6. THE GIRLS' SQUAD

1. Phụng's assertion here that Tuesday was not a day for sanitary visits does not match with the statements of contemporary French medical officials (see Charbonnier 1936, 41).

2. Joseph Jules Brévié (1880–1964) was a long-standing colonial administrator

who had previously served six years as governor general of French West Africa before serving in Indochina from September 1936 to August 1939.

3. Alfred de Vigny (1797–1863) was a prominent French poet and prose writer. A former military officer, in 1835 he published *Servitude et Grandeur Militaires* (Military Servitude and Grandeur), a set of three stories that realistically examined military life. Albert Sarraut (1872–1962) served as governor general of Indochina from November 1911 to January 1914 and January 1917 to May 1919. He later served as minister of colonies. A champion of colonialism's virtues, in 1931 he published *Grandeur et Servitude Coloniales* (Colonial Servitude and Grandeur), which articulated his vision of colonialism.

4. For the original French text, see Joyeux 1930, 633.

5. For the original French text, see Joyeux 1930, 638. Phụng's translation of the original is somewhat inaccurate as he does not include that prostitution involves selling the body to "all who come and without choice" (Joyeux 1930, 638).

6. For the original French text, see Coppin 1930, 571. Here again, Phụng took some liberties in his translation.

7. Edouard Daladier (1884–1970) was minister of war and national defense under the Popular Front government. A left-wing politician, he was prime minister at the time of writing the piece quoted. *L'Oeuvre* (Work) was a left-wing newspaper. There is no evidence it was run by Daladier as stated.

8. Madame Limongi, whose name Phụng incorrectly spells as Limongie in the text, had begun working in the Dispensary in 1936. Born in 1906, she was a Red Cross–trained nurse whose husband was a police officer (MH 929).

9. Lemur tunic is an early name for the *aó dài,* the long, flowing tunic now regarded as the national dress for Vietnamese women. The design was created by the Hanoi-based artist Nguyễn Cát Tường (1911–1946) in the mid-1930s. Embraced by many at the time as eminently stylish, it was vigorously opposed by some conservatives as being too risqué.

CHAPTER 7. WOMEN OF THE BOOK OF SORROWS

1. Jean-Etienne Dominique Esquirol (1772–1840) was an early French psychiatrist.

2. The Book of Sorrows *(Số Đoạn Trường)* can be described as a supernatural ledger wherein the fates of individual humans who are doomed to misfortune are written. It features prominently in *The Tale of Kiều* as the heroine Kiều's name is written in it, thus dooming her to the many misfortunes she encounters.

3. The pathogens for gonorrhea, syphilis, and soft chancre respectively.

4. 914, Gonacrine, and Dmelcos (mentioned below) were drugs used to treat venereal diseases.

5. A "lost" or "stray" cow *(bò lạc)* was a slang term used by Hanoi playboys for

girls who had just come from the countryside. "Certain" *(chắc chắn)* meant that the woman was still free of venereal disease.

6. "The willow character is misshapen…" refers to an out-of-wedlock pregnancy. The words are inspired by a line from a poem by the eighteenth-century female poet Hồ Xuân Hương that read, "Duyên thiên chưa thấy nhô đầu dọc."

7. All three lines come from *The Tale of Kiều*. "Seven tricks…" is from line 1210, when Tú Bà is instructing Kiều on how to successfully work as a prostitute. "Juice from a pomegranate rind…" is from line 837 and refers to procedures used to trick clients into thinking a prostitute is a virgin. "She'd change the flowers…" is from line 937 and refers to activities carried out by prostitutes with few customers to attract more.

8. Phụng incorrectly identifies Douguet as the Hanoi mayor. He was instead a senior official in the office of the resident superior of Tonkin. Phụng refers here to the directive that Douguet signed on behalf of the resident superior in August 1928 that describes the Dispensary's internal regime (see Joyeux 1930, 642–645). An earlier version of the internal regime that informed the 1928 legislation can be found in appendix 2.

9. Georges Clemenceau (1841–1929) served as prime minister of France from 1906 to 1909 and 1917 to 1920. He played a critical role in organizing the Allied victory in World War I. René Bérenger (1830–1915) was also a prominent French politician. He was elected to a lifetime Senate appointment in 1876, which he held until his death. A distinguished lawyer, he was a regulationist who was active in social affairs, notably in trying to eliminate the trafficking of women.

10. The passage running from "is it true" to "Clemenceau's idea stated" is missing from the Vũ Trọng Phụng 2000b version.

CHAPTER 8. MEDICAL EXAMINATION DAY

1. Phụng chose not to literally translate "sanitary visit" but instead opted for *ngày khám bệnh,* which is best literally translated as "disease examination day." I have chosen "medical examination day" as the best rendering of his meaning.

2. Mai Lan Phương was a male classical Chinese actor renowned for his portrayals of female characters.

3. "Đình Bảng, Cầu Lim, Phùng, Noi, etc." refers to women from rural northern Vietnam.

4. *Đời Mưa Gió* (A Turbulent Life) is a 1934 novel written by the prominent northern Vietnamese writers Khái Hưng and Nhất Linh. The story explores the complex relationship between Chương, a teacher at Hanoi's prestigious Lycée du Protectorat (School of the Protectorate or Trường Bưởi), and Tuyết, the daughter of an upper-class family who ends up working as a prostitute.

5. In a footnote in the original text, Phụng commented, "This way of address-

ing me was certainly used because I had used the title of correspondent for the paper *Tương Lai* in my investigations, and a small part of this piece had appeared in *Tương Lai* before it was banned."

6. *Maquillage* is a play on words as the French noun can be glossed as both applying makeup and fakery.

7. Kim Trọng is the name of Kiều's true love in *The Tale of Kiều*.

8. *Sapèques* are Vietnamese coins.

9. For the original French text, see Coppin 1930, 575–576.

10. For the original French text, see Joyeux 1934b, 903.

11. The Ducrey bacillus causes chancroids or soft chancre.

CHAPTER 9. STUDENT AND TEACHER

1. The full name of the organization was the Prophylactic League of the City of Hanoi (La Ligue Prophylactique de la Ville de Hanoi). According to the archival record, the governmental decision for its founding was approved on October 25, 1934 (RST 79707), though Joyeux listed the date as October 26, 1934. Phụng's discussion in this paragraph draws heavily from Ligue Prophylactique de la Ville de Hanoi 1937, 9.

2. In the text, Phụng includes the school's name in both Vietnamese and French. The former translation, however, is somewhat at variance from the original as it is translated as "School for Hygienic Male-Female Sexual Relations" (Vệ Sinh Nam Nữ Giao Cấu Học Đường). It is unclear whether the Vietnamese version was his or—the more likely case—that it was what he had read or heard at the Dispensary. The inclusion of "hygienic" *(vệ sinh)* in the Vietnamese version fits well with the health rhetoric common at that time.

3. Phụng quotes here from Ligue Prophylactique de la Ville de Hanoi 1937, 11.

4. Phụng shows his characteristic sensitivity to language in the paragraph by highlighting that the teacher referred to her students as "older sisters" *(các chị)*. Student-teacher relations in colonial Vietnam were very hierarchical, and a student would normally be referred to as "child" *(con)* or, in rarer cases, "younger sibling" *(em)*.

5. Phụng refers here to his 1934 *reportage, Kỹ Nghệ Lấy Tây* (The Industry of Marrying Europeans) (see also Vũ Trọng Phụng 2006).

6. Phụng makes the assertion here that the government must list her as eighteen, but this claim is contradicted by earlier reports from the Dispensary and the Service des Mœurs that listed women under eighteen. An accurate recording was necessary because underage women were not permitted to work as prostitutes and were to be returned to their natal locales.

7. Among the prostitutes with papers, a small number received permission to work outside of the brothels and set up in private residences by themselves. Like

the women working in brothels, they were still obliged to submit to weekly medical examinations. Paul Bert Street, which is today's Tràng Tiền Street, was the center of French colonial social life. Running between the Opera House and the southern shore of Hoàn Kiếm Lake, the street was lined with shops and cafés where French residents met and relaxed.

8. Lưu Linh is one of the Seven Sages of the Bamboo Grove who, in addition to being a poet and scholar, was a famed drinker.

CHAPTER 10. THE AUTHORITIES' PERSPECTIVE

1. Việt Sinh was the pen name of Nguyễn Tường Lân (1910–1942), an author who was more popularly recognized by another pen name, Thạch Lam. Lam was best known for his 1943 short volume *Hanoi's 36 Guild Streets (Hà Nội 36 Phố Phường)*. The full title of the *reportage* to which Phụng refers is *Hanoi at Night: A Reportage on Prostitution in Hanoi (Hà Nội Ban Đêm: Phóng Sự Về Nạn Mại Dâm ở Hà Nội)*. It was written by Việt Sinh and Tràng Khanh and published in eight installments in the newspaper *Phong Hóa* in 1933. The full text is available in Phan Trọng Thưởng, Nguyễn Cừ, and Nguyễn Hữu Sơn 2000, 1:685–705.

2. For the original French text, see Coppin 1930, 562.

3. Thăng Long, or "Rising Dragon," is an early name for Hanoi.

4. "Children of heaven" refers to China.

5. *Mousmés* is a French rendering of the Japanese word for daughter, *musume*.

6. For the original French text, see Coppin 1930, 570–571. The reference to the "old, dirty, repugnant and scabies-ridden" in the paragraph above is found in Coppin 1930, 570.

7. For the original French text, see Le Roy des Barres 1930, 595.

8. Quoted in Abadie-Bayro 1930, 533.

9. The origin of this quotation is unclear.

10. For the original French text, see Coppin 1930, 581–582.

11. For the original French text, see Virgitti and Joyeux 1938, 11.

12. For the original French text, see ibid., 11–13.

13. For the original French text, see ibid., 4.

14. Spirit mediumship *(hầu bóng* or *đồng bóng)* is a Vietnamese popular religious practice in which a medium invites spirits into his or her body so that the living can communicate with the spirits. Spirit medium rites always involve stylized dancing by the medium as part of the ritual structure.

15. "Female cavalry" or perhaps "cavalry women" *(nữ kỵ binh)* was a slang term used by the pleasure-seeking set to describe the dancing girls.

16. For the original French text, see Virgitti and Joyeux 1938, 13–17. The entire section on dancing girls is translated from Virgitti and Joyeux 1938, which indicates that Phụng received a version of the text before the 1938 printing.

17. Ibid.

18. Phụng uses three terms here *(cô gái, cô tây,* and *me tây)* that, while not exactly synonymous, were part of the discourse used to describe Vietnamese women in relationships with French men, particularly soldiers. He added the exclamation point to Coppin's text because, as his contemporary readers would have known, these women had been the subject of his earlier *reportage, The Industry of Marrying Europeans.*

19. For the original French text, see Coppin 1930, 581.

20. For the original French text, see Coppin 1930, 582.

21. The "meeting houses" in the original text are the *maisons de rendez-vous.*

22. For the original French text, see Joyeux 1930, 464.

23. For the original French text, see Coppin 1930, 583.

24. For the original French text, see Joyeux 1930, 465.

25. Henri Maspéro (1882–1945) was a famous French scholar of Vietnamese culture and history. His greatest scholarly fame was earned through his work on Taoism in China.

26. *Tiếu lâm* are humorous Vietnamese folk stories, often of an earthy or bawdy tone. François Béroalde de Verville (1556–1626) was a renowned French author.

27. For the original French text, see Coppin 1930, 565–567.

CHAPTER 11. HOLDING PAPERS

1. In this scene the prostitute Lành is playfully teasing Phụng, who is somewhat discomfited when she refers to him as "older brother" *(anh),* which would be normal with a client, but then addresses the hotel boy as "uncle" *(bác),* which asserts that the boy is of higher status than Phụng or that Lành is more concerned about staying on good terms with a boy who can bring her customers than she is with Phụng.

2. Phụng does not reveal whether he is using pseudonyms for the prostitutes, but the use of the name Lành, which in English means "gentle" or "sweet" when referring to a person, is likely a satirical jab at a woman he obviously does not like.

3. Colonial law required ambulant peddlers to have permits to sell their wares.

4. "Central" here refers to the Maison Centrale or Hỏa Lò Prison, the main prison run by the colonial authorities in Hanoi. It was located across the street from the Dispensary at the time of Phụng's writing.

5. Yến refers to the Dispensary here with the French term *dispensaire.*

6. Jean Valjean is the main protagonist in Victor Hugo's *Les Misérables.*

CHAPTER 12. TEARING UP PAPERS

1. In colonial Vietnam, it was common for people to have married by their late teens; thus the ages of the individuals Phụng describes were not exceptional.

2. Here, again, a teenager taking the primary school exam was not exceptional. Phụng, for example, passed his exam when he was fourteen.

3. For the original decree, see Joyeux 1930, 635.

4. *Maquereau* and *souteneur* are French words for pimp.

5. Phụng invokes here the Vietnamese adage *Lấy đĩ làm vợ, không ai lấy vợ làm đĩ.*

6. *Untel* is the French word for "So-and-So."

7. The characters for the woman's name are Thiên (heaven) and Kim (gold).

8. In this passage Phụng describes the proprietress of Thiên Kim's brothel as a 1937 version of Tú Bà, the madam in *The Tale of Kiều.*

9. Victor Basch was a prominent French intellectual who served as president of the League of Human Rights from 1926 to 1944. One of the guiding influences behind the formation of the Popular Front, he and his wife were murdered in 1944 by militia of the pro-German Vichy French government.

10. As Phụng explained in his own footnote, "According to common law or the common law regime [*régime de droit commun*], prostitution offenses would be brought before a court for trial and punishment and no longer handled by the Police des Moeurs or the dispensaries."

11. André Labrouquère was a left-leaning and politically active French scholar.

12. The provenance of this quotation is unclear. Henri Sellier (1883–1943) served as the minister of public health in the Popular Front government from 1936 to 1940.

13. Phụng noted in his own footnote, "According to that association, the list of countries that did not have brothels and the year that they closed their doors included Germany (1927), Denmark (1906), England (1901), Hungary (1928), Norway (1888), Holland (1911), Poland (1922), Sweden (1901), Bulgaria (1912), Saracen, Estonia, Finland (1907), Lithuania (1913), Czechoslovakia, the United States, India, Canada, Cuba, Australia, Bolivia, New Zealand, and the Dominican Republic" (quoted from Joyeux 1930, 501).

14. In the following section, up until the mention of Le Roy des Barres, Phụng draws heavily from Ligue Prophylactique de la Ville de Hanoi 1937, 17–20. Although not formally credited as the author on the pamphlet's cover, Joyeux wrote the text, and the Joyeux quotes Phụng includes in this section come from those pages.

REFERENCES

ARCHIVAL SOURCES

Hanoi Mayor's Office Files (MH)

MH 824. FRASS, Surveillante au Dispensaire. 1931–1937.
MH 870. Joyeux (Bernard). Directeur du Service Municipal d'Hygiène. 1929–1939.
MH 923. Le Roy des Barres (Adrien). Médicin des Services Municipaux et du Dispensaire. 1902–1912.
MH 929. Limongi (née Blanc Colombe). Surveillante Journalière du Dispensaire. 1938–1942.
MH 945. Mas (Félix). Agent de Police. 1918–1944.
MH 1127. Virgitti (Edouard Henri). Administrateur Maire. 1933–1938.
MH 2575. Internement de filles publiques au Dispensaire municipal. 1889–1890.
MH 2576. Plainte de Dumoutier a/s voisinage d'une maison de prostitution. 1893.
MH 2579. Prostitution clandestine. 1895–1938.
MH 2580. Rapport du Commissariat de police sur les maisons de tolérance sises à Hanoi. 1896.
MH 2583. Correspondances rélatives à la prostitution à Hanoi en 1910. 1910.
MH 2584. Rapports de la Police et lettres diverses au sujet de la Police des moeurs (prostitution) années 1913, 1914, 1915, et 1916. 1913–1916.
MH 2585. Correspondances rélatives à la prostitution à Hanoi. 1915–1916.
MH 2587. Correspondances rélatives à la prophylaxie des maladies vénériennes. 1917.
MH 2592. Rapport sur le fonctionnement du Service de contrôle médical et de réglementation de la prostitution surveillée à Hanoi. 1933.
MH 2593. Projet prophylactique des maladies vénériennes. 1938.

Resident Superior of Tonkin Files (RST)

RST 71907. Renseignements relatifs au fonctionnement du dispensaire de la ville de Hanoi. 1908.
RST 73684. Réglementation de la prostitution, dispensaires de Hanoi, Haiphong et autres. 1888–1913.
RST 78701. Mesures d'hygiène dans la ville de Hanoi. Arrêtés, règlements de police relatifs aux service des vidanges, au régime intérieur des dispensaires, à l'usage des fosses septiques. 1917–1937.

RST 79707. Dossier de la Ligue prophylactique de la ville de Hanoi. 1934–1937.
RST 79235. Construction d'un dispensaire à Hanoi. 1924–1925.

PUBLISHED SOURCES

Abadie-Bayro. 1930 (1915). "Morbidité Vénérienne des Troupes Européennes de l'Annam-Tonkin: Moyens Prophylactiques Proposés" (Venereal Morbidity of European Troops in Annam-Tonkin: Proposed Prophylactic Methods). *Bulletin de la Société Médico-Chirurgicale de l'Indochine* 6:525–561.

Bửu Hiệp. 1936. *La Médicine Française dans la Vie Annamite* (French Medicine in Annamite Life). Hanoi: Imprimerie Lê Van Phuc.

Charbonnier, Roger. 1936. *Contribution à l'Étude de la Prophylaxie Antivénérienne à Hanoï* (Contribution to Antivenereal Prophylaxis in Hanoi). Paris: Jouve.

Coppin, H. 1930 (1925). "La Prostitution, la Police des Mœurs et le Dispensaire Municipal à Hanoi" (Prostitution, the Police des Mœurs, and the Municipal Dispensary in Hanoi). *Bulletin de la Société Médico-Chirurgicale de l'Indochine* 6:562–593.

Corbin, Alain. 1991. *Le Temps, le Désir et l'Horreur: Essais sur le Dix-Neuvième Siècle* (Time, Desire, and Horror: Essays on the Nineteenth Century). Paris: Aubier.

Đào Duy Anh. 1996. *Từ Điển Hán-Việt* (Sino-Vietnamese Dictionary). Hanoi: Nhà Xuất Bản Khoa Học Xã Hội.

Gaide and Campunaud. 1930. *Le Péril Vénérien en Indochine* (The Venereal Peril in Indochina). Hanoi: Imprimerie d'Extrême-Orient.

Grenierboley, Jean. 1935. "Statistique 1934 de la Consultation de Vénérologie de l'Hôpital Indigène du Protectorat à Hanoi" (1934 Statistics of Venereology Consultations of the Hôpital Indigène of the Protectorate in Hanoi). *Bulletin de la Société Médico-Chirurgicale de l'Indochine* 1:52–54.

Grenierboley, Jean, and Nguyen Huu Phiem. 1943. *84 Schémas, Ordonnances, et Techniques Dermatologiques* (84 Diagrams, Prescriptions, and Dermatological Techniques). Hanoi: Imprimerie d'Extrême-Orient.

Guénel, Annick. 2001. "Prostitution, Maladies Vénériennes et Médecine Coloniale au Vietnam de la Conquête Française à la Guerre d'Indépendance" (Prostitution, Venereal Diseases and Colonial Medicine in Vietnam from the French Conquest to the War of Independence). In *Vietnamese Society in Transition*, ed. John Kleinen, pp. 233–249. Amsterdam: Spinhuis/IIAS.

Harsin, Jill. 1985. *Policing Prostitution in Nineteenth-Century Paris*. Princeton, NJ: Princeton University Press.

Hershatter, Gail. 1999. *Dangerous Pleasures: Prostitution and Modernity in Twentieth-Century Shanghai*. Berkeley: University of California Press.

Joyeux, Bernard. 1930. "Le Péril Vénérien et la Prostitution à Hanoi (État Actuel—Bibliographie—Règlementation)" (The Venereal Peril and Prostitution in

Hanoi [Current Conditions—Bibliography—Regulation]). *Bulletin de la Société Médico-Chirurgicale de l'Indochine* 6:453–514.

———. 1932. "Le Péril Vénérien en Indochine" (The Venereal Peril in Indochina). *Bulletin de la Société Médico-Chirurgicale de l'Indochine* 3:328–339.

———. 1934a. "Organisation de l'Hygiène et de la Protection de la Maternité et de l'Enfance Indigène à Hanoi" (The Organization of Hygiene and the Protection of Indigenous Mothers and Children in Hanoi). *Bulletin de la Société Médico-Chirurgicale de l'Indochine* 5:503–522.

———. 1934b. "Projet de Lutte Antivénérienne à Hanoi" (Draft of the Antivenereal Struggle in Hanoi). *Bulletin de la Société Médico-Chirurgicale de l'Indochine* 12:901–923.

Keller, Pierre. 1937. "De la Cécité au Tonkin" (Blindness in Tonkin). *Revue Médicale Française d'Extrême-Orient* 5:543–550.

Le Roy des Barres, A. 1924. *Rapport Annuel sur le Fonctionnement du Bureau d'Hygiène de la Ville de Hanoi, Année 1923* (Annual Report on the Operation of the Hygiene Bureau of the City of Hanoi, 1923). Hanoi: Imprimerie d'Extrême-Orient.

———. 1929. "Rapport Annuel sur le Fonctionnement du Bureau d'Hygiène de la Ville de Hanoi, Année 1928" (Annual Report on the Operation of the Hygiene Bureau of the City of Hanoi, 1928). *Bulletin de la Société Médico-Chirurgicale de l'Indochine* 12:692–715.

———. 1930 (1927). "Les Maladies Vénériennes au Tonkin" (Venereal Diseases in Tonkin). *Bulletin de la Société Médico-Chirurgicale de l'Indochine* 6:594–613.

———. 1931. *Le Cancer de la Verge* (Cancer of the Penis). Hanoi: Imprimerie d'Extrême-Orient.

Levine, Philippa. *Prostitution, Race and Politics: Policing Venereal Disease in the British Empire.* New York and London: Routledge.

Ligue Prophylactique de la Ville de Hanoi. 1937. *Le Dispensaire Antivénérien Municipal et la Ligue Prophylactique de la Ville de Hanoi* (The Antivenereal Municipal Dispensary and the Prophylactic League of the City of Hanoi). Hanoi: Imprimerie d'Extrême-Orient.

Lockhart, Greg. 1996. "Introduction: First Person Narratives from the 1930s." In *The Light of the Capital: Three Modern Vietnamese Classics,* trans. Greg Lockhart and Monique Lockhart. Kuala Lumpur: Oxford University Press.

Malarney, Shaun Kingsley. 2002. *Culture, Ritual, and Revolution in Vietnam.* Honolulu: University of Hawai'i Press.

———. 2006. "Health and Structural Violence in Colonial Indochina." *Journal of Social Science* 61 (March): 27–56.

Nguyễn An Nhân and Lê Trúc Hiên. 1933. *Nam Nữ Bí Mật Chỉ Nam* (Guide to Male-Female Secrets). Hanoi: Nhật-Nam Thư Quán Dược-Phòng.

Nguyễn Di Luân. 1932. *Nam Nữ Ái Tình* (Male-Female Love). Nam Định: My Thang.

Nguyễn Du. 1983. *The Tale of Kieu: A Bilingual Edition of Truyện Kiều*. New Haven and London: Yale University Press.

Nguyễn Văn Khai, trans. 1924. *Nam Nữ Hôn-Nhân Vệ-Sinh* (Male-Female Marital Hygiene). Haiphong: Imprimerie Typo-Lithographique Van Minh.

Nguyễn-võ Thu-hương. 2008. *The Ironies of Freedom: Sex, Culture, and Neoliberal Governance in Vietnam*. Seattle: University of Washington Press.

Phan Trọng Thưởng, Nguyễn Cừ, and Nguyễn Hữu Sơn. 2000. *Phóng Sự Việt Nam, 1932–1945* (Vietnamese *Reportage* 1932–1945). 3 vols. Hanoi: Nhà Xuất Bản Văn Học.

Riou, M. "Statistique Annuelle 1936 de la Consultation de la Clinique Dermato-Vénéréologique de l'École de Médicine d'Hanoi" (1936 Annual Statistics of Consultations at the Dermato-Venereological Clinic of the Medical School of Hanoi). *Bulletin de la Société Médico-Chirurgicale de l'Indochine* 1:129–131.

Rodriguez, Marie-Corine. 2001. "L'Administration de la Prostitution: Réglementation et Contrôle Social au Vietnam pendant la Période Coloniale" (The Administration of Prostitution: Regulation and Social Control in Vietnam during the Colonial Period). In *Vietnamese Society in Transition*, ed. John Kleinen, pp. 223–232. Amsterdam: Spinhuis/IIAS.

Spongberg, Mary. 1997. *Feminizing Venereal Disease: The Body of the Prostitute in Nineteenth-Century Medical Discourse*. New York: New York University Press.

Taraud, Christelle. 2003. *La Prostitution Coloniale: Algérie, Tunisie, Maroc (1830–1962)* (Colonial Prostitution: Algeria, Tunisia, Morocco (1830–1962). Paris: Payot.

Thao Thao. 1937a. *Gái Lục Sì* (Dispensary Girls). *Việt Báo,* February 16, pp. 1 and 3.

———. 1937b. *Gái Trụy Lạc* (Debauched Girls). *Việt Báo,* February 17, pp. 1 and 3; February 19, pp. 1 and 3; February 21, pp. 1 and 3; February 24, pp. 1 and 2; February 26, pp. 1 and 2; February 28, p. 1; March 3, p. 1.

Tô Linh Thảo. 1933. *Nam-Nữ Phòng Trung Bí-mật Tân Y Thuật* (New Medical Secrets of Male-Female Sexual Relations). Nam Định: My Thang.

Vaughan, Megan. 1991. *Curing Their Ills: Colonial Power and African Illness*. Stanford, CA: Stanford University Press.

Việt Sinh and Tràng Khanh. 2000. "Hà Nội Ban Đêm: Phóng Sự Về Nạn Mại Dâm ở Hà Nội" (Hanoi at Night: A *Reportage* on Prostitution in Hanoi). In *Phóng Sự Việt Nam, 1932–1945* (Vietnamese *Reportage* 1932–1945), ed. Phan Trọng Thưởng, Nguyễn Cừ, and Nguyễn Hữu Sơn, vol. 1, pp. 685–705. Hanoi: Nhà Xuất Bản Văn Học.

Virgitti, H., and B. Joyeux. 1938. *Le Péril Vénérien dans la Zone Suburbaine de Hanoi* (The Venereal Peril in the Suburban Zone of Hanoi). Hanoi: Imprimerie d'Extrême-Orient.

Vũ Trọng Phụng. 1938. *Một Hành Vi Bất Lương trong Nghề Phóng Sự và điều Tra* (A Dishonest Deed in the *Reportage* and Investigation Trade). *Chuyện đời* 5 (May 7): 3–5.

———. 1999 (1937). *Lục Xì*. In *Vũ Trọng Phụng: Toàn Tập* (Vũ Trọng Phụng: Complete Works), vol. 1, pp. 353–504. Hanoi: Nhà Xuất Bản Hội Nhà Văn.

———. 2000a (1936). *Làm Đĩ* (Prostitute). Hanoi: Nhà Xuất Bản Văn Học.

———. 2000b (1937). *Lục Xì*. In *Phóng Sự Việt Nam, 1932–1945* (Vietnamese *Reportage* 1932–1945), ed. Phan Trọng Thưởng, Nguyễn Cừ, and Nguyễn Hữu Sơn, vol. 1, pp. 771–876. Hanoi: Nhà Xuất Bản Văn Học.

———. 2002. *Dumb Luck*. Ann Arbor: University of Michigan Press.

———. 2006. *The Industry of Marrying Europeans*. Ithaca, NY: Cornell Southeast Asia Program Publications.

White, Luise. 1990. *The Comforts of Home: Prostitution in Colonial Nairobi*. Chicago: University of Chicago Press.

Zinoman, Peter. 2002. "Introduction: Vũ Trọng Phụng's *Dumb Luck* and the Nature of Vietnamese Modernism. In Vũ Trọng Phụng, *Dumb Luck*. Ann Arbor: University of Michigan Press.

singers' houses *(maisons chanteuses)*, 22–23,
116–117; clientele, 23; numbers, 23.
See also *ả đào* singers
Sisters of Saint Paul of Chartres, 10
Số Đỏ (Dumb Luck), 5
speculum *(mỏ vịt)*: anxieties toward use of,
18–19
suburban zone, Hanoi: characteristics of,
22; number of sex workers, 23. *See also*
Khâm Thiên Street; Patenôtre Treaty
of 1884
syphilis: epidemiological dimensions,
33–35; impact upon fertility and
infant mortality, 36–37, 56; treatment
with "914," 35

Tale of Kiều, The, 6, 26, 66, 83
Tam Lang, 3
Thao Thao, 11, 25, 29, 30–31, 32
Theron, Jules, 10, 33, 35
thousand-year civilization *(nghìn năm văn
vật)*, 17, 21, 47, 87, 88, 107
Tôi Kéo Xe (I Pulled a Rickshaw), 3

Vaughan, Megan, 2, 37
venereal diseases: epidemiological dimensions, 33–35; impact on prostitutes,
33–35, 93–94; main types, 33; treatments, 9, 30, 35, 83; use of Vietnam-

ese treatments, 33–35; Vietnamese
attitudes toward, 38, 57, 112
Việt Sinh, 4, 106
Vigny, Alfred de, 75
Virgitti, Edouard Henri, 13, 15, 22, 23, 45,
49, 52, 66–67, 74, 95
Vũ Trọng Phụng: attitudes toward "romantic" women, 26–27, 81, 103, 135,
150; attitudes toward speculum, 19;
biography, 2; condemnation of masturbation, 39–40, 84, 150; condemnation
of materialism, 23, 81, 84, 103; critique
of men and the prostitution problem, 26–27, 31–32, 81, 82; negative
consequences of modesty, 40–41, 97,
99; pornography allegations, 5; position on recruitment to prostitution, 5,
24–32, 81, 103, 127–128; prostitution
and moral failure, 23–27; prostitution
reform ideas, 149–150; racial anxiety
and disease, 37, 150; *reportages*, 3–4;
role of poverty in prostitution, 27–32,
127–128; on sexuality, 40–41, 97;
social consequences of ignorance,
33–41, 97, 147, 150; Westernization of
Vietnamese society, 84; women's liberation, 149–150

Zinoman, Peter, 3, 37

ABOUT THE TRANSLATOR

Shaun Kingsley Malarney received a B.A. in anthropology from Boston University and an M.A. and Ph.D., also in anthropology, from the University of Michigan. He has published extensively on the consequences of revolutionary cultural change in Vietnam and is the author of *Culture, Ritual and Revolution in Vietnam* (2002). He is presently professor of cultural anthropology at International Christian University in Tokyo.

OTHER VOLUMES IN THE SERIES

HARD BARGAINING IN SUMATRA:
Western Travelers and Toba Bataks in the Marketplace of Souvenirs
Andrew Causey

PRINT AND POWER:
Confucianism, Communism, and Buddhism in the Making of Modern Vietnam
Shawn Frederick McHale

INVESTING IN MIRACLES:
El Shaddai and the Transformation of Popular Catholicism in the Philippines
Katherine L. Wiegele

TOMS AND DEES:
Transgender Identity and Female Same-Sex Relationships in Thailand
Megan J. Sinnott

IN THE NAME OF CIVIL SOCIETY:
From Free Election Movements to People Power in the Philippines
Eva-Lotta E. Hedman

THE TÂY SƠN UPRISING:
Society and Rebellion in Eighteenth-Century Vietnam
George Dutton

SPREADING THE DHAMMA:
Writing, Orality, and Textual Transmission in Buddhist Northern Thailand
Daniel M. Veidlinger

ART AS POLITICS:
Re-Crafting Identities, Tourism, and Power in Tana Toraja, Indonesia
Kathleen M. Adams

CAMBODGE:
The Cultivation of a Nation, 1860–1945
Penny Edwards

HOW TO BEHAVE:
Buddhism and Modernity in Colonial Cambodia, 1860–1931
Anne Ruth Hansen

Production Notes for Vu / *Luc Xì*
Cover design by Julie Matsuo-Chun
Interior design and composition by Wanda China with display type in
    Ptarmian Condensed and text in Garamond Premier Pro
Printing and binding by Edwards Brothers, Inc.
Printed on 35 lb. EB Natural, 360 ppi